How do you get the most benefit from all seventeen Rules to Live By? Easy. Just remember that all of us have a pretty large collection of bad habits that weaken our chance to succeed in life. Each of the rules you will learn will help you to get rid of a bad habit by replacing it with a good one. *That's your key to a better life*. Concentrate on just one rule per day. None of the rules are very long. Longevity is not a necessary requirement for value or truth. Read the rule in the morning, follow its guideline throughout the day, put a tiny check mark on the page, and then move on to the next rule on the following morning.

By the time you have moved through all seventeen rules, you may decide to go through them again. Wonderful!

The plan is simple, but it's all up to you. Persist, give it a fair chance, and soon you will discover that many of your old bad habits that have been holding you back are gradually being replaced by good habits, life-changing habits. What to do then? *Share* what you have learned, just as I have shared myself, and my life, with you.

Only then will you realize what success and a better way to live truly means.

—Og Mandino
From *A Better Way to Live*

D0051331

Bantam Books by Og Mandino

A BETTER WAY TO LIVE
THE CHOICE
THE CHRIST COMMISSION
THE GIFT OF ACABAR (*with Buddy Kaye*)
THE GREATEST MIRACLE IN THE WORLD
THE GREATEST SALESMAN IN THE WORLD
THE GREATEST SALESMAN IN THE WORLD,
  PART II: The End of the Story
THE GREATEST SECRET IN THE WORLD
THE GREATEST SUCCESS IN THE WORLD
MISSION: SUCCESS!
OG MANDINO'S UNIVERSITY OF SUCCESS
THE RETURN OF THE RAGPICKER

A BETTER WAY TO LIVE

Og Mandino

BANTAM BOOKS
NEW YORK · TORONTO · LONDON · SYDNEY · AUCKLAND

A BETTER WAY TO LIVE
A Bantam Book
Bantam hardcover edition / February 1990
Bantam paperback edition / January 1991

All rights reserved.
Copyright © 1990 by Og Mandino.
Cover design copyright © 1990 by One Plus One Studio.
Cover photo copyright © 1990 by Don Giannatti.
Library of Congress Catalog Card Number: 89-17950.
No part of this book may be reproduced or transmitted
in any form or by any means, electronic or mechanical,
including photocopying, recording, or by any information
storage and retrieval system, without permission in
writing from the Publisher.
For information address: Bantam Books.

If you purchased this book without a cover you should be aware that this book is stolen property. It was reported as "unsold and destroyed" to the publisher and neither the author nor the publisher has received any payment for this "stripped book."

ISBN: 978-0-553-28674-8

Published simultaneously in the United States and Canada

Bantam Books are published by Bantam Books, a division of Bantam Doubleday Dell Publishing Group, Inc. Its trademark, consisting of the words "Bantam Books" and the portrayal of a rooster, is Registered in U.S. Patent and Trademark Office and in other countries. Marca Registrada. Bantam Books, New York, New York.

PRINTED IN THE UNITED STATES OF AMERICA

OPM 35 34

For two very special grandchildren,
Danielle and Ryan
. . . and their parents,
Carole and Dana

A BETTER WAY
TO LIVE

Part One

LESSONS FROM MY PAST

I learned this, at least, by my experiment; that if one advances confidently in the direction of his dreams and endeavors to live the life which he has imagined, he will meet with success unexpected in common hours.

—THOREAU
Walden

Choice! The key is choice. You have options. You need not spend your life wallowing in failure, ignorance, grief, poverty, shame, and self-pity!
There is a better way to live!

—MANDINO
The Choice

I

There was only one other customer in Don June's Scottsdale barber shop, and he couldn't help overhearing my announcement to Don that I was finally "golfed out" and ready to commence work on my next book, one that would be based primarily on material from keynote speeches that I deliver many times each year to corporate and association conventions.

In all my writing and speech-making throughout the years, I am forever reminding my audiences that, like the laws of nature, gravity, and physics, the true principles of success have been with us for thousands of years. *They have never changed!* And these old principles will always work for you—or against you—no matter how you are trying to live your life.

Unfortunately, we're living in an age that often seems to be traveling faster than the speed of light. We're all looking for fast answers to our problems . . . easy solutions . . . quick fixes . . . free lunches . . . elevators to success . . . and this futile search for a philosopher's stone that will somehow magically transform our daily efforts into trunks of gold has blinded us to the old laws that have always worked and always will work. Even though they're still right under our noses, we no longer recognize them . . . and so they have become "secrets." How sad.

Although I planned, in the new book, to introduce and then explain these ancient principles and how they could be applied by my readers to change their lives, almost immediately, for the better, both my publisher, Bantam Books, and I felt that we should have a different title than "The Greatest Secrets of Success," which is how my speech has always been billed and promoted. But what? Several agonizing weeks passed while we tossed ideas around with little progress.

For most authors, writing without a title is no big deal. They just forge ahead with their work, confident that sometime before they complete the book, a year or more in the future, either they or their publishers are certain to come up with something provocative enough for that cover page. Not me. I've always needed a title first—a banner around which I could rally my thoughts and feelings constantly, not only when I was at the typewriter but also when I was away from it.

Commencing with *The Greatest Salesman in the World,* in 1967, I've always known the title of all thirteen of my books before I ever typed the first sentence of Chapter One, and since that procedure has worked well enough to sell more than twenty million volumes, in eighteen languages, I wasn't about to alter my routine in any way. And then, as has happened so many times in my life, fate, chance, luck, coincidence, God (call it what you will) intervened and resolved my problem.

After that other barber-shop customer paid for his haircut, he hesitantly approached my chair, where Joan was already doing my nails, and said, "Mr. Mandino, I think your books are great. I'm a dentist, and I give courses in self-esteem to other members of the dental fraternity, which, for reasons we still don't completely comprehend, has one of the highest suicide rates of any profession in the nation. I use many of your books to reinforce the guidelines on living that I teach."

I mumbled some words of appreciation as he was opening the front door. He paused before stepping outside, turned back, and said, "My favorite book of all you have written is *The Choice*."

I grinned and nodded. "There was a lot of me in that one."

"I rather thought so. Would you be open to a suggestion from this unabashed fan of yours?"

"You bet!"

"Well, in the *The Choice*, your hero walks away from corporate life and writes a book with a great title that becomes a smash best-seller. I wish you would seriously think about writing a book with that very same title. Perhaps you might even consider it for this new book you were just discussing with Don. Then you could take the rules and suggestions for a more fulfilling existence that your hero wrote and spoke about in that book and combine them with the many other old principles and secrets of success that you have dealt with in all your other works and speeches for so many years. Do that and you most certainly would produce a very special volume that could help millions escape from their prisons of drudgery and unhappiness. Just make it simple and easy for us to use and follow—a modern *Book of Life*, if you will."

As he disappeared into the bright Arizona sunshine, I'm certain that I was at least a foot out of the barber's chair. Maybe more. I couldn't wait for Don to finish his cutting and trimming, and I'm positive I exceeded a few speed limits racing up Scottsdale Road on my way home to phone my Bantam editor, Michelle Rapkin.

"Another title?" was her greeting.

"This is it, lady. Now I'm ready to go to work!"

"Tell me," she said anxiously.

"I'm going to borrow the fictitious title given to a fictitious book by a fictitious character created by Og Mandino . . ."

". . . who is definitely not fictitious!" Michelle exclaimed.

I took a deep breath. "I'm going to call the new book *A Better Way to Live*!"

Michelle phoned back late that afternoon. The reaction from Bantam's executives was unanimous approval!

That stranger making contact with me in a barber shop and providing me with the title of the book you are now holding—fate, coincidence, luck, chance . . . ?

Let's take it another step. There are approximately fifty-five thousand new books published each year, and there were probably twenty thousand different titles, both hardcover and paperback, in the store where this book was purchased. And yet, of all the books *you* could be reading at this very moment, *you* are holding *A Better Way to Live*.

Fate, coincidence, luck, chance . . . ? I don't think so. I am convinced that many times, in the course of our lives, God challenges us with a golden opportunity, a seemingly impossible hurdle, or a terrible tragedy . . . and how we react— or *fail* to react—determines the course of our future, almost as if we were involved in some sort of heavenly chess game . . . with our destiny always in the balance.

Is this only a chance meeting between you and me? I don't believe it. As the wise old British poet Samuel Taylor Coleridge wrote a long time ago, "Chance is but the pseudonym of God for those particular cases which he does not choose to acknowledge openly with his own sign-manual."

We have been brought together for some special reason, we two. Let's make the most of it.

II

Now that we know you and I will be spending some time together, I suggest we do it right here in my studio, the room that my kids call "Dad's word factory." I'll sit where I'm always sitting when I'm in here, at my desk, and during your visits you can relax in that old wing chair facing me.

I'll talk, for the most part, and you listen. Okay?

Remember Henry David Thoreau's admonition in his great classic *Walden*? He told us that if we have built castles in the air, our work need not be lost, for that is where they should be. Then he urged us to put foundations under them.

I am going to share with you some powerful tools that you can use, not only to construct your castles, but also to erect their permanent substructure. You're about to learn how to turn many of your dreams into reality. But . . . you must listen with an open mind and an open heart and then be prepared to *act*. All the noble thoughts, magnificent plans, and "secrets" of achievement in the world are of little value unless and until they are put into action. Our worth is always determined by our deeds, not by our good intentions, however noble.

Several years ago, while touring the nation to

promote one of my books, I appeared on a television show in Houston. As soon as I had settled in my seat onstage and the audience applause had subsided, Steve Edwards, the show's host, held up my latest book and asked, "Og, what will this new book of yours do for me?"

Fair question, but I was still taken aback by Steve's straightforwardness. No one, on all the programs in all the cities, had hit me with that one. I hesitated for a moment, collected my thoughts, and finally replied, "Probably not very much, Steve. After all, it's just a collection of pulp, ink, glue, and fiber, and if you take it home this evening, read it from cover to cover, and awake tomorrow morning expecting your life to be miraculously changed for the better, you will have wasted both your time and your money."

Steve grinned and leaned back in his chair, almost as if he knew what was coming next. I then went on to explain, to Steve and to his audience, the three conditions necessary to get full value and benefit from any quality book written to teach, motivate, or inspire.

First, you must be willing to admit that there are one or more categories of your life—career, marriage, goals, finances, self-esteem, happiness, children, to name just a few—where things could certainly stand some improvement. This is not difficult. None of us have attained divine perfection. Even though we may fool others, we can never really hide the truth from ourselves. We know where we're lacking.

Now, having made some sort of mental tally of the debits in your life, you have put yourself in the proper, receptive frame of mind necessary to extract full value from the self-help book you are reading, whether it was penned by Peale or Gibran or Maltz or Hill or Stone . . . or Mandino, perhaps. How? By accepting the possibility that the author just may have something valuable to share with you that perhaps he or she has acquired through many years of study, experience, and observation. And of course it doesn't hurt your adviser's credentials if there happen to be a few million satisfied readers as references.

One more condition. Grit your teeth, if you must, and admit to yourself that the path on which you have been traveling in your search for happiness, success, wealth, peace of mind, or whatever, doesn't seem to be leading anywhere, while the pages of your life seem to be turning at a faster and faster clip. If you can willingly accept that synopsis of your affairs, if your way just has not been working, then ask yourself what you have to lose if you follow some ideas and suggestions from Og that might, *just might,* enable you to discover a better way to live for you and those you love.

I want a genuine commitment from you, a sincere promise that you will really work at the principles I'm going to share with you. No lip service . . . and no false pride. Remember that nobody makes it alone. All of us need help to grow, to achieve, or to recover from disaster. No man or woman is an island. There is absolutely no such person as a self-made man or woman, so, please, let me help you.

You might be too young to remember her, but Lillian Roth was a superb entertainer who, several decades ago, saw her career drown in a sea of booze. Years after her tragic downfall, the gripping story of Roth's struggle with alcohol was graphically told in a powerful book and film entitled *I'll Cry Tomorrow*. In many of her subsequent interviews she confessed, again and again, how absolutely powerless she had been in trying to overcome her problem until she was finally able to utter three little words: "I need help!"

We all need help! Nobody makes it alone, and I often recall in my speeches the partially apocryphal but poignant tale of Albert and Albrecht Dürer that my late friend and mentor Louis Binstock, revered rabbi of Chicago's Temple Shalom, shared with me many years ago.

Back in the fifteenth century, in a tiny village near Nuremberg, lived a family with eighteen children. Eighteen! In order merely to keep food on the table for this mob, the father and head of the household, a goldsmith by profession, worked almost eighteen hours a day at his trade and any other kind of paying chore he could find in the neighborhood. Despite their seemingly hopeless condition, two of Albrecht Dürer the Elder's children had a dream. They both wanted to pursue their talent for art, but they knew full well that their father would never be financially able to send either of them to Nuremberg to study at the academy.

After many long discussions at night in their crowded bed, the two boys finally worked out a pact. They would toss a coin. The loser would go down into the nearby mines and, with his earnings, support his brother while he attended the academy. Then, when that brother who won the toss completed his studies, in four years, he would support the other brother at the academy, either with sales of his artwork or, if necessary, also by laboring in the mines.

They tossed a coin on a Sunday morning after

church. Albrecht Dürer won the toss and went off to Nuremberg. Albert went down into the dangerous mines and, for the next four years, financed his brother, whose work at the academy was almost an immediate sensation. Albrecht's etchings, his woodcuts, and his oils were far better than those of most of his professors, and by the time he graduated, he was beginning to earn considerable fees for his commissioned works.

When the young artist returned to his village, the Dürer family held a festive dinner on their lawn to celebrate Albrecht's triumphant homecoming. After a long and memorable meal, punctuated with much music and laughter, Albrecht rose from his honored position at the head of the table to drink a toast to his beloved brother for the years of sacrifice that had enabled Albrecht to fulfill his ambition. His closing words were, "And now, Albert, blessed brother of mine, now it is your turn. Now you can go to Nuremberg to pursue your dream, and I will take care of you."

All heads turned in eager expectation to the far end of the table where Albert sat, tears streaming down his pale face, shaking his lowered head from side to side while he sobbed and repeated, over and over, "No . . . no . . . no . . . no."

Finally, Albert rose and wiped the tears from his cheeks. He glanced down the long table at the faces he loved, and then, holding his hands close to his right cheek, he said softly, "No, brother. I cannot go to Nuremberg. It is too late for me. Look . . . look what four years in the mines have done to my hands! The bones in every finger have been smashed at least once, and lately I have been suffering from arthritis so badly in my right hand that I cannot even hold a glass to return your toast, much less make delicate lines on parchment or canvas with a pen or brush. No, brother . . . for me it is too late."

More than 450 years have passed. By now, Albrecht Dürer's hundreds of masterful portraits, pen and silver-point sketches, watercolors, charcoals, woodcuts, and copper engravings hang in every great museum in the world, but the odds are great that you, like most people, are familiar with only one of Albrecht Dürer's works. More than merely being familiar with it, you very well may have a reproduction hanging in your home or office.

One day, to pay homage to Albert for all that he had sacrificed, Albrecht Dürer painstakingly drew his brother's abused hands with palms together and thin fingers stretched skyward. He called his powerful drawing simply "Hands," but the entire world almost immediately opened their hearts to his great masterpiece and renamed his tribute of love "The Praying Hands."

The next time you see a copy of that touching creation, take a second look. Let it be your reminder, if you still need one, that no one—no one—ever makes it alone!

Of course, *you* don't have to try to make it alone. Whether your faith is great or almost nonexistent, you still have your own set of praying hands. All you need do, whenever things get tough, is just touch your palms together, extend your fingers, raise your eyes, and say, "I need help." I've done it at least a thousand times in my life. Results? You might be surprised when you discover how close help is if you just ask for it.

For now, it's you and me. That other special help will always be there for you, believe me, but you've only got me for a little while . . . so let's get on with this rewarding project of changing your life for the better.

III

Now, before you test the comfort of that old chair, let me give you a hasty tour of this room where I spend so much of my time. I want you to feel completely at ease with me, and perhaps the best way to get you in that frame of mind is by walking you around this cluttered space that is filled with so many books, keepsakes, photos, mementos, and relics of my years. Hopefully, as you view and touch a few souvenirs of my life, you will begin to look upon me as an old and trusted friend, and it will then be much easier for you to accept my ideas.

Careful where you step. Those are stacks of new books that I expect to read in the next few months, and next to them, on the carpet, are several book manuscripts recently sent to me by authors, both friends and strangers, seeking testimonials. I find it almost impossible to turn them down, and yet, if I'm not careful, I can spend all my waking hours doing nothing but reading manuscripts and writing complimentary sentences for book jackets.

See this stack of long sheets on the top of the pile? That is a recently received set of galley proofs for a new book titled *Impartial Judgment* written by an old friend, National Football

League referee Jim Tunney. I've just sent his publisher my testimonial.

Few people, even close friends, are allowed in this studio. Yes, *you* are special. However, several years ago during a party, Jim was standing right about where you are now, and he was staring at my desk and typewriter with a strange expression on his face. Puzzled, I finally asked, "Jim, what's wrong?"

The only man who has ever refereed three Super Bowls, with all their tremendous pressure and responsibility, just kept shaking his head and smiling faintly. "Nothing is wrong, Og," he almost whispered. "I'm picking up such powerful vibes just being in this special room where all those great characters you write about come alive for the first time. Wow! Someday . . . someday . . . I'm going to write my book!"

Jim never lost sight of his dream. It took a while, but this is what his "someday" looks like— galley sheets for a book that will, I'm certain, become a best-seller.

As you can see, the walls, blinds, drapes, carpet, and upholstery in this room, located in the southwest corner of our home, are all in tans, browns, and blacks. When my wife, Bette, was trying to help me select colors, she said that it really didn't matter what we picked for this room, since she knew I'd have all available space covered with memorabilia of one sort or another before long. As you can see, she was correct.

This so-called studio of mine, close by the kitchen and pantry, measures only 12' x 19'. Whenever I begin to feel crowded, I just remind myself that the entire interior of the house that my favorite author, Thoreau, built near Walden Pond was only 10' x 15', and he never complained about lack of room.

That wall to your left, as you entered, is my "braggin'" place. Since even the cleaning lady stays away from this room (at her request), I don't feel too self-conscious about the ostentatious display you see before you. Actually, I'm very proud of every item hanging there. This is the Napoleon Hill Gold Medal that I received in 1983 for literary achievement, and next to it is the lovely plaque that was presented to me when I became the thirteenth individual inducted into the International Speakers Hall of Fame a year later. Below them, as you can see, is a large collage created by Bette, made up of more than forty family photographs, all fitted together in a lovely mosaic of our years. It hung in my Chicago office during all the years I headed *Success Unlimited* magazine.

Moving along, I'm sure you recognize most of the subjects in these framed photos autographed to me—Jimmy Stewart, Norman Vincent Peale, Michael Jackson, Joey Bishop, Frank Gifford, Rudy Vallee, Art Linkletter, Chuck Percy, Robert Cummings, Colonel Harland Sanders, Ed Sullivan, W. Clement Stone, and Napoleon Hill. Quite a mix!

That 1919 *Saturday Evening Post* cover depicting a golfer sneaking out of his office with his clubs on his shoulder is from my oldest son, Dana, and below it are framed certificates attesting to my listing in *Who's Who in America* and *Who's Who in the World* as well as my membership in the Organization of Amazing Men, inclusion in the

Library of Human Resources of the American Heritage Research Association and the National Speakers Association's Council of Peers Award of Excellence, the highest speaking honor the association bestows.

The most important and priceless award displayed on that wall, however, is that framed drawing with accompanying letter put together by my younger son, Matt, for a second-grade project, fifteen years ago. In large block letters, as you can see, MY DAD is printed on buff cardboard, and beneath the words is a drawing of a man with a baseball hat, wearing a large glove and with a bat at his feet. All this is on a pedestal that reads: "The Most Valuable father award to Mr. Mandino from his son." The letter to the right of the drawing proclaims the following:

by Matt Mandino

the most Valuable father

He was elected for this award for playing catch with me when my brother would't. He is Quite a good athlete for a 50 year old man. Once he climbed a 6 foot fence to play baseball with me in the field. And he got a baseball down from the roof. One time I was trying to get my kite up in the air but I could't do it so when he came home he got it so high it got tangaled up on a telephone wire. I don't know about you but I think my father is the greatest.

Matt

Pasted between the drawing and the letter is a ribbon marked Award of Excellence from Matt's teacher. When Matt finally brought it home and presented it to me, I could not have been prouder. I hugged him, and I guess I cried a little. That shook him up.

On this low bookcase, beneath all those pictures and awards, are thirty-plus years of boxes of photographs, slides, and albums, plus a couple of cameras, and on the floor is another pile—framed awards and citations lovingly given to me by groups and associations that I have recently addressed. There's just no more room on any of these walls, as you can see, but somehow I can't bring myself to pack them away.

That three-shelf bookcase next to the corner is filled with books dealing with the life of Christ. These are only a tiny percentage of all the volumes I read during the ten years I was researching the book that eventually became *The Christ Commission*. Toughest book I ever wrote. I shall be forever grateful to the United Press International for praising it with the words "one of the freshest and most original approaches to the soul of Christianity written in a long time."

Those two file cabinets in the corner once contained, among other things, the original copies of all my book manuscripts; but I finally got smart, and they are now stored in a vault. Butting up against the windowsill on this south wall is a long, low table that, at the moment, holds a carton destined for the garage, of old newspaper clippings and articles about me, a world globe that I love lighting up, two small oil landscapes from friends, an unopened LP album, *I Can Hear It*

Now/The Sixties, narrated by Walter Cronkite, several large color enlargements of Matt and Dad on the golf course, a color photo of my brother, Silvio, in uniform, inscribed with love "To Og, My favorite commanding officer," a large Bible, and several cassettes sent to me by fellow speakers to critique.

Hanging on that wall, next to the window, is a photo of me and my B-24 crew before we commenced our thirty-mission combat ordeal over Germany in 1943, my certificate of promotion to the rank of first lieutenant, a three-dimensional plaque of Dürer's "The Praying Hands," a large silver scroll that needs polishing, engraved to Og Mandino from the Sales and Executive Club of Guadalajara, an authentic autographed photo of Charles Lindbergh, my first hero, posing next to his plane, *The Spirit of St. Louis,* and a framed calligraphic antique parchment of "The Salesman's Prayer" from my book *The Greatest Salesman in the World.*

No, I don't own a word processor, yet. This vintage 1965 IBM on the desk extension has typed all thirteen of my books, although I did write the first draft of *Greatest Salesman,* in 1966, on a portable Olivetti, which I still have, before we could save enough money to buy this second-hand Selectric.

Resting on my desk is an unframed copy of a painting of Jesus by Ralph Pallet Coleman. It was a gift to me, almost fifteen years ago, from the chaplain of Scottsdale Memorial Hospital. Note that the pose is of Jesus resting His arms on a table, His hands clasped as if He were the chairman of the board calling a meeting to order. I write at night, often from ten to dawn, and for many years I have always placed my palm lightly on the face of Jesus, whenever I finish, and whisper, "Good night, Boss," just before I turn the lights out.

Attached by Scotch tape to the wall above my desk is a strip of photos of Matt and Dana mugging for an arcade camera when they were young, a Polaroid shot of Dana with his lovely wife, Carole, and their children, Danielle and Ryan, whom I adore, a gorgeously engraved multicolor mint one-peso Mexican note now worth 1/2500 of a dollar, a thank-you letter to Mom and Dad from Matt when he moved away from home and into an Arizona State University dormitory, and a letter from Bette that I found one morning propped up on my typewriter after I had spent several anguished nights and days making little progress on a book. Yes, of course you can read it. I've already cleared it with her.

1/18/80

Hi!

I love you!

Don't let yourself get down. Yesterday was just "His" way of telling you He wants you to take a different approach.

Just relax. He'll provide a map with a very clear route. You're not His only problem.

Keep the faith . . . and He'll be back to you shortly.

Never let us down before . . . don't start doubting Him now.

Have a super day.

Your Betsie

With support like that, it's difficult to fail.

Yes, I know, that "In" basket on the left corner of my desk is stacked high with mail. Always is. I receive, on the average, slightly over a hundred letters each week from people who have read one of my books. I answer every one myself, even if it's only a few brief lines of thanks for the nice things the sender wrote. I've always felt that if someone cares enough to write, they deserve an answer from me, personally—not from a secretary, and certainly not a form letter. I've always derived deep satisfaction from the mail, although many of the letters tear at my heart when so many of God's lovely people graphically and honestly describe how low they had fallen before one of my books entered their life and helped to turn things around for them. I save every precious letter. They're all stacked in cartons out in the garage. Pack rat.

Also on this desk are file folders containing information on my next several speeches . . . in New York, Seattle, Boston, Mexico City, Toronto, Dallas. I limit myself to just two speeches a month, and try to deliver a new book to my publisher every two years. The rest of the time I really do smell the roses . . . and I'll show them to you, later, in the backyard. Lots of them.

Facing me on this desk is a sepia print of a wedding pose of my beloved mother and father, a foot-high ceramic statue, made by Bette, of a little guy in a baseball uniform with CHICKS on his chest, the name of Matt's first Little League team, a Rolodex, a large calendar with both my appointments and speech bookings for most of this year and some of next already marked in, several legal pads, a DO IT TODAY! list, file cards everywhere, a telephone with a Cobra answering machine, a photo of Dana coaching a soccer team of young ones and one of Matt coaching his 1987 Little League championship team.

Next to my typewriter is a small tape recorder and a stack of white typing paper. I use more than four thousand sheets before completing a book—and fill my wastebasket many times. Also within reach, at all times, is *Webster's New Collegiate Dictionary* and *Roget's Thesaurus.* The west wall is to my back when I write, and below its only window is another bookcase filled with reference books that I tap frequently, such as the University of Chicago's *A Manual of Style,* Adler and Van Doren's *Great Treasury of Western Thought, The New Dictionary of Thoughts,* Strunk and White's *The Elements of Style,* and *The Timetables of History.* On the floor are several telephone books and my two briefcases. The fatter one only travels with me when I'm working on a book.

In the corner to my left is the old overstuffed chair that was occupied for many years, whenever I was working at this typewriter, by my loving basset hound, Slippers, to whom I dedicated *The Greatest Salesman in the World, Part II, The End of the Story.* I miss him very much even though he's been gone almost two years. Yes, that's an old bone of his still on the seat cushion.

Books, five rows high, cover the entire north and final wall of this room, dealing with every possible subject from religion to motivation, from investing to mental health. The top of this long bookcase through the years has become a repository for hundreds of objects meaningful to me. I'll just point out a few for now. Here is a copy of the first issue of *Success Unlimited* magazine that I edited in 1965, and next to it is an unframed oil painting from a prisoner depicting what he conceived that Simon Potter, the ragpicker hero in my book *The Greatest Miracle in the World*, might look like. This tiny pair of sneakers belonged to Dana, and next to them is a small pair of leather thongs that Matt wore when he was four. Here is a photo of me getting a haircut while I autographed books in a Fairhope, Alabama, bookstore, my old passport, a tarnished pair of my bombardier's wings, a 1984 pass to the original Skins Game at Desert Highlands Country Club, one of Matt's first teeth that the tooth fairy replaced with a quarter, name badges from countless conventions where I have spoken, a sawed-off handle from a Little League bat, a color photo of a lovely park in Guatemala City where I addressed a capacity crowd several years ago, a loving message to me from a young lady fan who eventually died of leukemia, an invitation to W. Clement Stone's eightieth birthday party, a photo of a beautiful and loving nun, Sister Maria Bernardo, embracing me when I arrived to autograph my books in a Manila bookstore, several small Bibles, plastic geraniums that continue to arrive from many who have been touched by *The Greatest Miracle in the World*, a Michigan number plate that reads SUCCES, Father's Day cards from my two boys, a badge commemorating the tenth annual Glenn Miller festival in Clarinda, Iowa, a proclamation from the mayor of Lima, Ohio, declaring July 27, 1981, as Og Mandino Day, an old stereoscope, the two worn IBM typewriter printing balls that typed the words for my first eleven books, a scrapbook of dried flowers from the Holy Land, and more pictures of my family. And hanging on the wall above, all the way to the ceiling, are plaques and trophies and award certificates, including the National Quality Award for underwriting excellence in the life-insurance industry dated (God help me!) 1954.

In front of where you will be sitting is a table with stacks of books, videotapes, and scores of reels of Super-8 movie film that I have shot during the past twenty years and that I am slowly editing for conversion to videotape. My only problem is that I can't bring myself to discard very much footage from any of the movie reels, since they all hold precious memories that I don't want to end up in the wastebasket. Consequently, we are assembling a rather extensive family videotape library. Beneath all those film reels the table itself is a huge and striking chessboard with inlaid wooden squares that Matt artfully constructed when he was a high-school freshman. It deserves a much better spot than this.

On your left, near the doorway, are more plaques and a framed copy of the farewell article that I ran in *Success Unlimited* when I announced my retirement, in 1976, at the age of fifty-two, to just "take things easy." Very funny! Since then, I have delivered more than four hundred speeches in fourteen countries and written eight books, and I'm on my third set of golf clubs.

See this framed Polaroid photo near the doorway? It has a very special place on my wall . . . and in my heart. Several years ago I received a letter from a distraught mother who wrote that her young son was dying from brain cancer and had only a few months to live. He had just finished reading *The Gift of Acabar*, which I had co-authored with Buddy Kaye, and asked his mother if she would buy him copies of the book to give to his twelve closest buddies "so that they would always remember him." Mother was writing to ask . . . if she sent the books to me, would I autograph them to his friends? Then Dougy would also sign them before distributing them.

I responded immediately. All I wanted were the names, and I'd take care of the rest, which I did. Such a small gift for such a brave little guy.

The Gift of Acabar, if you have not yet read it, relates the story of a young crippled lad in Lapland who, during the long months of seasonal darkness, built a huge red kite and flew it high in the sky to catch a star that he could haul down to earth in order to illuminate his poor village. He succeeds . . . and the star, named Acabar, talks to him and teaches him much about life before being returned to the heavens, in a special way, when the sun reappears in the spring.

Dougy, God bless him, miraculously remained alive for almost two years longer than expected. And then one day I received the letter from his mom that I had been dreading for so long. With the letter was this Polaroid photo she had taken of his tiny headstone. Next to that stone, see the curled dark wire extending several feet above the grave, and on top of the wire is a red kite . . . a red kite embracing a star!

I am such a fortunate man. To be able to sit here at this typewriter and touch people like Dougy is such a miracle that whenever I ponder it for very long I get frightened, even at my age.

Finally, here's a hanging cloth poster, right under the light switch, that Bette presented to me long ago. I still like its sentiment: "God grant me patience . . . and I want it right now!"

Feeling more at home now?

Good. Have a seat, kick off your shoes, and lean back. Let me reach out and help you. . . .

IV

Picture this scene for me, if you will.

It's a wet and gray and dismal morning in one of the most desolate and dangerous neighborhoods of Cleveland. With the thermometer hovering just above the freezing mark, the earlier downfall of snow has changed into a combination of rain and ice, and the refuse-strewn streets and gutters, with their endless rows of dingy bars, porno peep shows, and smelly hamburger joints, are almost empty of humanity. One would search in vain for even a small hint that it is only four weeks to Christmas.

Suddenly, we see movement . . . a sign of life. Leaning against a cracked pawn-shop window, to protect himself from the elements, is a derelict, his tattered denim shirt providing little protection from the cold and wet for his thin body. The wretch's matted hair hangs down to his shoulders, his eyes are bloodshot from the cheap wine he has already consumed this morning, and his stomach aches from lack of food.

After his bearded face has been pressed against the dingy pane of glass for several minutes, something inside the pawn-shop window, on the drab and dusty shelf, catches the bum's attention. A gun . . . a small handgun, and attached to it is a yellow tag: $29.

The man moans and jams his bruised right hand into the pocket of his soiled jeans, removing three soggy ten-dollar bills—all he has in the world. Then he cries out, half-aloud, "There's the answer to all my problems! I'll buy that gun and a couple of bullets and take them back to that mangy room where I'm staying. Then I'll load the gun, put it to my head . . . and pull the trigger! And never again . . . never again . . . will I have to face that terrible failure in the mirror!"

That man was indeed a failure. He had managed, in just a few short years, to lose everything in life that was precious and meaningful to him—a loving wife, a beautiful daughter, a nice home, a decent job, plus all his pride, his faith, his confidence, and his self-esteem. He had tried to play the game of life—as so many do—without taking the time to learn the rules. And now he was about to pay the price for his ignorance. In the rain, on that miserable morning, he was ready to throw his life away.

That pitiful human being, preparing to cancel his future, was not about to perform an unusual act. Sadly, I'm afraid, that same scenario is repeated hundreds of times every day in this beautiful country of ours when people finally lose their last shred of hope in a tomorrow that once held so much promise. And that doesn't count the thousand who don't take their lives but give up anyway. They quit on themselves. They let all their dreams fade into the twilight. They stop trying and just exist, leading what Thoreau called "lives of quiet desperation." They're already dead, at age twenty-five or thirty or forty or even fifty, for all they're accomplishing . . . even though we won't get around to burying them until they're seventy-two.

Fortunately, that sorry individual, that loser shivering in the rain in Cleveland, didn't buy that gun. He didn't blow his life away on that terrible morning so many years ago.

If he had, I wouldn't be here to share these precious moments with you . . . or to help you make your dreams come true.

V

Heartbreak, tragedy, financial embarrassment, love lost, termination of employment, divorce, promotion bypass, defeat, lack of education, feelings of inferiority, drugs—these are only some of the spears from an impartial fate that can wound you for a day, a week, a month, a year.

But you can deal with any affliction, and change those conditions in your life for the better, once you are able to convince yourself that life never was, and never will be, 365 days of sunshine, ice cream, laughter, and music. As President Kennedy said, "Life isn't fair. It never was and never will be." Even the most successful people, the most acclaimed and honored individuals in the world, have had to survive chapters of failure and hopelessness.

Why didn't I buy that handgun and end my life? No guts, probably. Even the sorry act of suicide requires a sliver of courage, and I had fallen so low, and was in such a terrible condition mentally, that I couldn't even bring myself to put an end to my misery.

I guess it's quite natural—and after all these years of writing and lecturing I expect it—that whenever I'm being interviewed by the press or on radio and television, I'm always being asked the same questions, year after year. How did you manage to turn your life around so dramatically? What did you do that raised you from the gutter to the presidency of a national magazine in less than ten years? Where did you, such a loser, with only a high-school education, gain the wisdom and knowledge that has enabled you to write so many best-sellers? And what secrets of success (they still insist on calling them "secrets") did you learn that might help others who feel discouraged and defeated to reach a better life?

Travel back in time with me. . . .

I was blessed with a spunky freckle-faced Irish mother and a hard-working Italian immigrant father whose talents as a gardener kept his family from starving, on many occasions, during the Depression years. Mother, despite our near-poverty situation, had a dream for her first child, and she had me convinced, long before I ever began school, that someday I would be a writer. "And not just a writer," she would always hasten to remind me, "a great writer!"

I bought her dream. Being a "great writer" was okay with me, and in order to please Mother I was already writing short stories and reading grown-up books during my primary grades while the other kids were struggling with the Dick-and-Jane basal readers. We held fast to our dream all through school, and in my senior year at Natick High School, in Massachusetts, I served proudly as the news editor for our school paper, *The Sassamon*. Finally, after spending months reviewing scores of college catalogs, Mother and I decided that the school of journalism at the University of Missouri was the best place for me, and we proceeded with our plans. During my high-school graduation ceremonies, in the town's only movie house, my folks listened proudly when their son was introduced to read the Class Will he had written.

Two months after the June 1940 graduation, while my mother was making lunch for me one day in our little kitchen, her blessed heart stopped beating, and she died before my eyes. That was the end of our dream. Instead of attending any college, I quickly enlisted in the army air force, qualified as a bombardier, and eventually flew thirty combat missions with Jimmy Stewart's B-24 group, the 445th.

I returned from the war in 1945, and discovered very quickly that there wasn't much of an employment market for bombardiers with only a high-school education. Didn't bother me much. I had managed to earn a pair of silver wings before I was old enough to vote, not to mention several combat decorations, and so I was convinced that I could do just about anything.

Although London partying, between missions, had managed to drain most of my monthly flight officer's pay, I still had more than nine hundred dollars when I went to New York City, after separation from the air force, and boldly rented a cold-water flat just off Times Square. Then I went out and bought a secondhand portable Smith-Corona and some writing supplies. It was not too late to fulfill my mother's dream. I would still be a writer . . . a great writer!

I failed. For the next six months, after setting up shop in my cockroach-infested kitchen, I must have visited at least fifty magazines whose offices were within walking distance, but none showed much interest in my stuff. I left copies of articles, short stories, a few poems, even clever fillers, but the mailman never delivered a single check. Finally, when my savings were all but drained, I gave up on our dream again, returned to Boston, and applied for the veterans' "52–20" Club, which paid honorably discharged GIs twenty dollars per week for fifty-two weeks. Eventually, after scores of painful and frustrating interviews, I was hired as an insurance-agent trainee for a large national company. They "trained" me for four days, and then turned me loose on the coastal town of Winthrop, as a debit agent, that now-outmoded individual who once called on homes each week to collect insurance premiums. Soon I was married, and we purchased an old two-family house under the GI Bill. Thus began ten of the most terrible years of my life . . . for me and those unfortunate enough to be closest to me.

The treadmill I soon found myself on was torture. Never was I more than a few paces ahead of several bill collectors, and making the monthly mortgage payments was a major challenge despite my long hours of work. I would go anywhere, at any time, to try to sell a policy, and still there were always more bills than money to pay them. Then God blessed us with a lovely daughter, and I struggled even harder to make good. To no avail. Even though my wife finally went back to work, we just kept slipping deeper and deeper into debt.

One night, after failing to close on an insurance prospect, I stopped at a bar on the way home for a drink. God knows I deserved it . . . didn't I? It had been a long, tough day, and I had just struck out on what I had expected to be a sure sale that would have earned me more than sixty dollars— dollars I needed so desperately—as an initial commission. Soon that one drink, on my trips home in the evening, became two . . . then four . . . then six . . . and through my thoughtless actions, over a period of many months, I managed to destroy the love of the two people in the world who meant the most to me. I made their lives, both my wife's and my daughter's, a living hell. It is no fun to cope with a drunk.

Finally, I paid for my unforgivable behavior. I returned home one Sunday from an insurance convention that had been held at Bretton Woods, New Hampshire, and on the kitchen table was a brief note. My wife and daughter had fled. They had suffered all they could from their sorry imitation of a husband and father. Two years later I was informed that my wife had been granted a divorce and custody of our daughter.

What followed my wife and daughter's departure was to be expected, I guess. Having driven away the only people in the world who loved me, the self-pity and boozing increased until I was no longer able to hold my job. Then, with no money coming in, I lost our home, and one morning I tossed what few clothes I possessed in the back of my old red Falcon automobile and hit the road. It was a terrible moment, driving away from our old neighborhood for the last time.

During the next several months I drank my way across the country, doing any kind of work I could find in order to survive and keep that cheap wine flowing. I drove an oil truck in Texas, worked on a construction crew in Oklahoma, was a pin boy in a bowling alley in Long Beach and a busboy in a Howard Johnson restaurant in Columbus—a thirty-five-year-old busboy!

Then there was Cleveland . . . several nights in drunk tanks, and finally, on that cold morning in the rain, a beckoning handgun in a pawn-shop window. I don't know what happened outside that store. I heard no voices, no harps playing, nor did I see any blinding flashes of light proclaiming my salvation. All I remember is that I turned away from that pawn-shop window, walked up the street in the rain, and staggered into a welcome shelter that was warm and dry . . . the public library.

Books, thanks to my mother's influence, had always been my friends, and so I began to spend much of my time, again, in that quiet and peaceful haven, searching for some answers. Where had I gone wrong? What could I possibly do with my life? Was it too late for this thirty-five-year-old drunken failure? I knew there was a better way to live, but where were the directions to locate that paradise?

During the following months, as I drifted eastward in my old jalopy, I spent as much time as I could, between my odd jobs, in local libraries, searching, reading, thinking. Aristotle, Carlyle, Peale, Emerson, Franklin, Plato, Carnegie, and a host of other wise men became my companions and my mentors. My drinking gradually tapered down to only an occasional beer, I acquired some new clothes, and my self-esteem gradually began to surface again, even though I still had no steady job. And then, on one wonderful and glorious morning, in Concord, New Hampshire's main public library, I discovered a book that changed my life forever!

Success Through a Positive Mental Attitude by W. Clement Stone and Napoleon Hill was so unlike most of the current "success" books of that era, which usually promised, on garish jackets, miraculous changes in your life, generally within thirty days and after just one reading. Stone and Hill's message was loud and clear: *You can accomplish anything you wish that is not contradictory to the laws of God or man, providing you are willing to pay a price.* Pay a price for your dreams. That was the difference between this book and the others. There was no free lunch. I devoured the book, read and reread it countless times, until I had almost memorized all the "Thoughts to Steer By" at the end of each powerful chapter.

Then, another gift from God. While I was studying and learning from Stone and Hill's great book, I met a very special lady and fell in love. She inspired me so much that I finally mustered enough courage to travel to Boston and apply for a salesman's job in W. Clement Stone's New England insurance company, called Hearthstone Insurance. To my great surprise and wonder, they hired me! They were willing to take a chance on this thirty-five-year-old loser, and soon afterward I married Bette. We are still together . . . and still in love.

This time, having been trained and motivated properly, I became a successful salesman with Hearthstone, quickly earning more money each week than I ever had in my life. Within a year I was promoted to sales manager, in the Northern Maine territory, where I recruited a hungry and ambitious group of young men, many right off potato farms, and soon we were attracting national company attention with our sales results. After being down for so long, I felt wonderful, and I reveled in the glory and recognition, but still . . . still . . . my mother's dream and mine kept surfacing. To be a writer . . . to be a great writer!

Finally, I bowed to my instincts, took a week off, rented a typewriter, and wrote a sales manual on how one could better sell insurance to the people in rural areas using W. Clement Stone's success principles. After rewriting it many times, I typed it as neatly as I could, bound it all in a brown folder, and mailed it to Mr. Stone's home office, in Chicago, with prayers that someone back there might actually read my work and realize what a great writing talent they had, buried in Northern Maine. Someone did . . . and within a few months Bette and I, with our new and first son, Dana, were moving to Chicago, where I was assigned to work in the sales-promotion department writing material for incentive programs and bulletins. At last I was writing!

In 1954, with Napoleon Hill, W. Clement Stone had founded a magazine titled *Success Unlimited*. Although there were a few thousand outside subscribers, the periodical had been used, during its first ten years of publication, primarily as a house organ for Stone's insurance conglomerate, and each month it was packed with countless motivational articles along with a sales piece, and often an editorial, by Stone. After working in sales promotion for nearly two years, I learned that the editor of *Success Unlimited* was about to retire. So I applied for the job, even though I didn't know a magazine galley sheet from a roll of toilet paper. However, what I lacked in knowledge and experience I made up for with my enthusiasm and newly acquired positive mental attitude, and in our interview I managed to convince Mr. Stone to give me the job. Og Mandino, executive editor. Wow!

I learned, quickly, that I had bitten off nearly more than I could digest. At that time the entire staff of the magazine was a part-time secretary and a layout artist. And so I was back, once again, to long, long working hours in order to put our tiny magazine together each month. It was all worthwhile. Within ten years we had a staff of 50, and the monthly paid circulation had grown from 2,000 to 155,000, a pretty fair percentage increase.

During that first year of struggle, one month I came up an article short for the issue we were putting together, and there was nothing in our file of available articles that pleased me. This, in retrospect, was just another example (there have been so many in my life) of God challenging me by moving His chess piece and then sitting back to see how I would handle it. Up to that time I had been so busy each month just putting the next issue together that there had been no time to try my hand at an article. However, when I realized I needed an article, *and I needed it the very next day or we'd miss our printing deadline,* I went home and wrote all night. My subject was the great golfer Ben Hogan, who had suffered through an automobile accident so nearly fatal that he was told he'd never walk again. Hogan not only *walked* again, he won the National Open again! Special man. I ran my piece in the magazine, and once more fate . . . coincidence . . . God (?) came into play.

A New York publisher got a toothache and visited his dentist. While sitting in the waiting room, he picked up off the coffee table the issue of *Success Unlimited* that contained my Hogan piece.

He read it, and when he arrived in his Park Avenue South office that afternoon, he wrote me a letter. The letter, in essence, was telling me that he believed I had considerable talent, and if I ever decided to write a book, he wished I would contact him.

Eighteen months later, Frederick Fell Publishing brought out my little book titled *The Greatest Salesman in the World*. Now, twenty-one years later, that book has become the best-selling book of all time in the field of sales in the entire world, with more than ten million copies in print in eighteen languages!

Within four years of the book's publication its sales had topped 350,000 in hardcover, and at that point Bantam Books was considering purchasing the paperback rights. The amount that Fell was asking for the rights was a sum beyond my comprehension in 1973: $350,000. However, before Bantam would agree to that price, the firm's executives wanted to meet with the author to assure themselves that he could be promoted as well as the book. And so, with my heart in my mouth, I boarded a plane for New York. Bette and I now had a second son, Matthew, and our growing family's future was hanging in the balance as I nervously rode the elevator up to the publisher's giant boardroom on Fifth Avenue. By the time I was finally ushered into the wood-paneled room packed with humanity, my knees were shaking and my voice was cracking. Combat missions were a lot easier.

For more than an hour I answered questions from various Bantam executives as best I could; the questions covered every possible subject, from my schooling, or lack thereof, to my plans, if any, for future books. I held my own until Oscar Dystel, then the chairman of Bantam and still a friend to this day, rose from his position at the head of the huge table, walked down to where I was sitting, grinned, extended his hand for a firm handshake and said, "Congratulations, Og, we've just bought your book." No vote, no request for a show of hands, no discussion. That was it.

I couldn't wait to finish with all the formalities and handshakes so that I could get back to my room at the New York Hilton to call Bette with the good news. I guess I was almost running by the time I emerged from Bantam's elevator, and I had gone no more than fifty yards on bustling Fifth Avenue when the heavens opened and we were hit by a horrendous lightning storm, with frightening claps of thunder resounding down that famous street. I had no topcoat to protect me from the downpour, and so I raced up the steps and inside the nearest beckoning doorway . . . that of a lovely church. I was alone inside, and the only sounds were the rain on the roof, intermittent thunder, automobile horns, and an organ, or a recording of an organ, playing "Amazing Grace," coming from the basement.

It happened yesterday, I'm certain. I can still relive every detail of those next precious moments so clearly. I remember walking slowly up to the front of the church, falling down on my knees, and sobbing. Then I clenched my hands tightly together, raised my head, and cried out, "Mom, wherever you are, I want you to know . . . we finally made it!"

VI

There! Now you know a lot more about me than I do about you.

Then again, perhaps I know more about you than you think I do.

One of the painful prices we are paying for our so-called modern life-style in the final quarter of this twentieth century is that we are all becoming more and more alike. We all suffer through the same television shows, read the same magazines, wear the same fashions, and buy the same new frozen foods. We all live, and die, by the clock, cut each other off in similar-looking automobiles, pass up a night at the ball game for a night at the office, never seem to have much time for our spouses or kids, watch helplessly as our oceans and lakes are poisoned, and try not to think of a hydrogen bomb landing anywhere near our city or town.

We are all, as the years pass, falling in step in order to march to the beat of the *same* drummer, racing forward or backward at the same pace as all others, smiling almost on command—mass-produced beings with no more individuality than any of the millions of saltine crackers that emerge, daily, from the ovens of Nabisco.

What is this mass conformity doing to us as we enter the robot age when the robots are not manufactured machines . . . but *us*? How's this for a sorry statistic? *More than three hundred thousand individuals in this beautiful country of ours attempt to take their lives each year!* Here are a couple more: *Over five million* prescriptions for Valium are dispensed in this country *every month*, and we are now treating *more than four thousand* new cases of mental illness *every twenty-four hours!*

We are even flushing ourselves down the drain in some sort of hysterical and desperate lockstep. The number of heroin and cocaine and "crack" and "speed" addicts is growing too swiftly to tally and is already at epidemic proportions, while we also now consume more booze, per capita, than at any time in history.

There must be a better way to live.

In the early seventies, soon after I had brazenly embarked on a second career as a motivational speaker because of the success I had enjoyed with my first three books, I learned a lesson one evening that has had a powerful effect on my writing and speaking ever since.

I had just stepped off the stage after receiving a rousing and exuberant standing ovation from a wonderful group of typically enthusiastic Amway representatives, and I was now in the theater lobby autographing my books. As the hour grew late and the line short, a young woman timidly approached my table and placed one of my books carefully before me.

As I was signing my name, she leaned forward and spoke softly, as if she wanted no one else to hear. "Mr. Mandino, I truly enjoyed your speech tonight but . . . but . . ."

I forced a weary smile. "But what?"

"Well," she replied, bowing her head, "you talked a lot about success, and you had some good points, but you made it all seem too easy. That's probably because you've never had to suffer through much failure and sorrow, and so you don't really understand what it's like to have to struggle from the bottom of the pile."

I was exhausted, but I still didn't sleep a wink that night. Never even bothered to undress. Just paced the floor in that hotel room, berating myself for my stupidity. My audiences, and my readers, had absolutely no idea where I was coming from, no knowledge of my background, because I had been too ashamed to let all those sorry details about my early years become public in any of my promotional material or book-cover copy. Only a few close friends knew that I had crawled out of the gutter and discovered a better way to live only after years of horror and pain and tears. Once more, God had moved a chess piece in my life. That soft-spoken and well-meaning Amway lady had delivered the message. I got it!

Within a week I had rewritten my entire speech, and when I went on a national tour to promote the paperback edition of *The Greatest Salesman in the World* for Bantam Books, I spoke without hesitation, on radio and television and to the press, about my early not-so-glory days. I wanted to make myself an example. I wanted the listener or viewer or reader to consider the Mandino story and then think, "If he can turn his life around, with the little he had to work with, then, by God, so can I."

Ever since then, in several hundred speeches, I have never walked out onstage to address an audience without boldly telling them the story of that sorry failure standing in the rain, contemplating suicide. Later, when I confess to them, as I did to you earlier, that the bum was me, there is usually a large gasp that passes through the crowd. They didn't know. So many still don't know. Then I inform them that from my past experience with other groups I was very certain that whether they were top executives, salespeople, small-business owners, teachers, athletes, parents, even students, I knew—I positively knew—that there was someone in my audience—at least one—who was feeling the walls closing in at that very moment, and although he might be smiling on the outside, he was dying on the inside, even as I spoke . . . and perhaps he, or she, was even close to giving up on life, as I was long ago.

At that point—and I still do all of this in my talks today—I would look around at the crowd and say, "Mr. X . . . or Mrs. X . . . or Miss X . . . wherever you may be out there, let me toss out a few life preservers and let's see what happens."

Gradually, as the years went on, I began to experience a strange phenomenon. When I first spoke out to the anonymous X person, usually at least one individual, following the speech, would shyly approach me, and while I was signing a book would say quietly, "I'm your Mrs. X . . . or Mr. X . . . or Miss X."

Without realizing it, I gradually developed a routine. When I would hear those words, I would reach out and hug that person, male or female. Then I would say, "A new beginning!", and the person would smile, nod, and reply, "A new beginning! Thank you!"

During the last four or five years, these "X" people have come forward to introduce themselves in ever-increasing numbers. More and more they, and all the rest of us, are being hammered into a life-style we cannot endure, cannot afford, and cannot cope with. We have forgotten one of the basic facts of life: When we were given dominion over this world, we were also given dominion over ourselves. We each plot our own map. God is not our navigator. It was never His intention to chart a course for each of us and thus place us all under His bondage. Instead, He bestowed on each of us intellect and talent and vision to map our own way, to write our own Book of Life in any manner that we choose.

You, sitting there—my audience of one. Can it be? Are you possibly one of my "X" people reaching out for a life preserver of your own? Hang on . . . you're too precious to lose. During my combat flying days, each morning before we flew a mission over Germany, we were briefed in detail on all the problems we might encounter and how to deal with them. We'll do the same, you and I. Before we part company, I will have briefed you on all you need to know to make your mission a success and enjoy a better way to live.

The secret, of course, is *choice*. You have options in your life. We all do. You need not spend another day wallowing in failure, grief, poverty, shame, or self-pity. Why are there so many failures—unhappy failures—everywhere one looks? The answer is simple, even if not obvious. Those who live in unhappy failure—even you, perhaps—have never exercised their options for the better things in life because they have never been aware that they had any choices!

But you do have choices—and, together, you and I are going to review many great life-changing options that are still available, choices that you can begin acting upon immediately, no matter what your present condition may be, so that you can begin to live a better life.

Albert Camus, the great French novelist and playwright, once said that every man, on the foundation of his own sufferings and joys, builds for all. The greatest lesson that I have learned in my sixty-plus years of suffering and joy is that life is a game. It's spiritual, mysterious, and precious, but it's still a game—and *you can't play in that game with any chance at all of winning unless you know the rules*!

Slight problem: Nobody ever taught you and me the rules when we were growing up. Not once—not in primary school, junior high, high school, college, or graduate school were we ever instructed on the simple but powerful techniques we needed to know in order to set goals and reach them, handle adversities, eliminate our bad habits, make friends, accumulate wealth, motivate ourselves and others, generate enthusiasm, and handle stress—to name just a few of life's challenges and hurdles. And so, sadly, most of us became spectators in the greatest game of all, shunted to the bleachers for a lifetime of watching and envying the successful ones—and we even had to pay to get in!

Okay, let's take inventory. Did you possibly acquire any skills during all those formative years of schooling that could help you to change your life for the better if you began applying it right now, today?

You bet you did! You learned how to read! With that great ability alone, the ability to read, you are about to work wonders with your life.

Remember when your elementary-school teachers printed instructions on the upper corner of the blackboard pertaining to recess, lunchtime, cloak-room order, fire drills, and so many other guidelines to help you get through the day? Well, regardless of your age, let's pretend that you're my pupil and I'm sharing with you a set of very important rules, not merely to get you through the day, although that's a good thing in itself, but the rest of your life. A rule, according to *Webster's New Collegiate Dictionary*, is a "prescribed guide for conduct and action." Perfect. Much better than the sterner sound of law or commandment, especially since some of the principles for a better way to live are merely suggestions and ideas, not uncompromising injunctions or life-or-death restrictions on your daily behavior.

How do you get the most benefit from all seventeen of the following *Rules to Live By?* Easy. Just remember that all of us have a pretty large collection of bad habits that weaken our chance to succeed in life. Each of the rules you will learn will help you to get rid of a bad habit by replacing it with a good one. *That's your key to a better life.* Concentrate on just one rule per day. None of the rules are very long. Longevity is not a necessary requirement for value or truth. Read the rule in the morning, follow its guideline throughout the day, put a tiny check mark on the page, and then move on to the next rule on the following morning.

By the time you have moved through all seventeen rules, you may decide to go through them again. Wonderful! As you make progress, day by day, you will soon discover that the rules are not independent of each other. Actually, many of them interlock in purpose and action, so that while you are concentrating on one, you are improving in several other areas simultaneously, and that makes this project to change your life for the better much easier than you expected.

Let what follows become your own personal Book of Life. The plan is simple, but it's all up to you. Persist, give it a fair chance, and soon you will discover that many of your old bad habits that have been holding you back are gradually being replaced by good habits, life-changing habits. What to do then? *Share* what you have learned, just as I have shared myself, and my life, with you.

Only then will you realize what success and a better way to live truly means.

Part Two

RULES TO LIVE BY

There are probably words addressed to our condition exactly, which, if we could really hear and understand, would be more salutary than the morning or the spring to our lives, and possibly put a new aspect on the face of things for us.

How many have dated a new era in their lives from the reading of a book? The book exists for us perchance which will explain our miracles and reveal new ones. The at present unutterable things we may find somewhere uttered.

These same questions that disturb and puzzle and confound us have in their turn occurred to all wise men; not one has been omitted; and each has answered them according to his ability, by his words and his life.

—THOREAU
Walden

I

RULE ONE . . . for a Better Way to Live

Count your blessings. Once you realize how
valuable you are and how much you have
going for you, the smiles will return, the sun
will break out, the music will play, and you
will finally be able to move forward toward
the life that God intended for you . . . with
grace, strength, courage, and confidence.

One of the most important and ageless secrets
of life that I had to learn, with pain and tears, is
that you cannot even begin to turn a hopelessly
bruised and defeated existence around or jump off
that dreary treadmill so far as your job and career
are concerned or move off that financial dead end
that seems to have doomed you to failure and low
self-esteem until *you appreciate the assets you already possess.*

Assets? You're smiling? Sad smile. Are you
trying to tell me something? You say you've got a
drawerful of bills? Your oldest child, perhaps, is
getting ready for college, and you don't have the
heart to tell her that she can't go? You're two
months behind on the car payments, and the job
seems none too secure. What assets, you're think-

ing? Stay with me now, while I help you to count some of your blessings, right this very moment, as you sit there feeling sorry for yourself.

Let's make a list, and let's try to put a dollar value on just a few of the good things in your life so that you realize how wealthy you really are and how much you have going for you, even though, in your daily struggle to survive, you may have forgotten this.

What's it worth to live in this great country? Go ahead, I dare you to put a price tag on that. Where would you rather live?

What would it be worth to be associated with the fine company you represent if you were standing in an unemployment line this morning?

What's your career worth when you realize that probably 95 percent of the world's population would gladly give up ten years of their life, or more, to have your opportunity.

What's your freedom worth?

How about those you love and who love you? How much would you take to give them up?

Your eyes? Would you take a million dollars for your eyes?

How about your hands or your feet? Five million dollars? Ten million?

You're really quite a precious specimen, aren't you? If it came to a showdown, you probably wouldn't trade what you have, right now, for all the gold in Fort Knox, would you? And with so much going for you, tell me, please, why you're walking around looking sad, beat, defeated, and rejected? Why?

No more! There is a better way to live for you, and it begins today. . . .

RULE ONE . . . for a Better Way to Live

Count your blessings. Once you realize how valuable you are and how much you have going for you, the smiles will return, the sun will break out, the music will play, and you will finally be able to move forward toward the life that God intended for you . . . with grace, strength, courage, and confidence.

II

RULE TWO . . . for a Better Way to Live

Today, and every day, deliver more than you
are getting paid to do. The victory of success will be half won when you learn the
secret of putting out more than is expected
in all that you do. Make yourself so valuable
in your work that eventually you will become indispensable. Exercise your privilege to go the extra mile, and enjoy all the
rewards you receive. You deserve them!

I thoroughly enjoy browsing through all the
humorous greeting cards that seem to be getting
more and more rack space in most card shops, and
I probably send out more of them than I should.
My all-time favorite was the oversize card with an
engraved border that looked like a stock certificate on which were embossed the words "How to
Make Money." Inside there were just three words,
in a brilliant Day-Glo orange: GO TO WORK!
Everything in life has its price, and unless
you belong to that tiny elite who have had everything handed to them since birth, I'm afraid the
only way you can pay for the things you want and

need and dream about is with the compensation you receive for the work you do.

You're nodding in agreement, but you don't look happy. Struggling to stay ahead of the bills? Not making much progress or growth in that job, and you've already been at it much too long without any advancement? You'd like a new house but can't afford it? Same with that clunker you're driving? Your life seems to be on a holding pattern; how do you get off the treadmill?

There is an answer, a solution, a rule, and I'll wager that it has never failed for those who have truly applied it. When it comes to improving the career side of your life, the greatest secret of success was delivered to us from a mountaintop, nearly two thousand years ago, when Jesus told us that if we were compelled to go a mile with someone, we should always go two. The extra mile.

If you resolve, beginning tomorrow, to put out more on your job than you're getting paid to do, miracles will begin happening in your life. Whatever you are doing for a living, whether you're selling products, painting houses, manning computers, or sweeping floors—if, each day, you do more than you're getting paid for, your life's pattern will soon change for the better.

The most certain way to condemn yourself to a life of failure and tears is by doing only the work covered by your paycheck. Of course, putting out more than you're expected to deliver will not make you very popular with some of your peers who seem to make a career out of doing as little as possible for their pay . . . but that's their problem, not yours. You live your life. There are people who are depending on you. When you give more than you're getting paid to give, every day, you will not only promote yourself, but by being indispensable you will discover, to your surprise, that new opportunities are all around you, and eventually you'll be able to write your own price tag. Such a simple rule. Go another mile! Won't cost you a cent, and yet it's so powerful that when you follow it, you will change your life forever.

Andrew Carnegie said that there were two types of people who never achieve very much in their lifetime. One is the person who won't do what he or she is told to do, and the other is the person who does no more than he or she is told to do. And when Walter Chrysler was asked what his plant needed most, he replied, "Ten good men who can't hear the whistle blow or read the time on the face of the clock."

Surprise everyone. Change your work habits. Go the extra mile! This does not mean sacrificing your family or your health in an insane drive for success, but it is a marvelous method for you to extract all that life has to offer and all you deserve. Work as though you would live forever, and live as though you would die today. Go another mile!

RULE TWO . . . for a Better Way to Live

Today, and every day, deliver more than you are getting paid to do. The victory of success will be half won when you learn the secret of putting out more than is expected in all that you do. Make yourself so valuable in your work that eventually you will become indispensable. Exercise your privilege to go the extra mile, and enjoy all the rewards you receive. You deserve them!

III

RULE THREE
. . . for a Better Way to Live

Whenever you make a mistake or get knocked down by life, don't look back at it too long. Mistakes are life's way of teaching you. Your capacity for occasional blunders is inseparable from your capacity to reach your goals. No one wins them all, and your failures, when they happen, are just part of your growth. Shake off your blunders. How will you know your limits without an occasional failure? Never quit. Your turn will come.

One of the most misunderstood great truths from the past has echoed down the centuries, and yet only the wise heed its advice. *If you want to succeed, you must learn to live with failure.* We learn wisdom from failure much more than from success. Show me the person who has never stumbled, never messed up a job, never made a mistake, and I'll show you a person with a very dim future.

Mistakes, blunders, defeats, are unavoidable in this rough-and-ready life, but if we let them make us gun-shy, so that once we get knocked down we hesitate to try again, we're condemning ourselves to a life of regret. The very best lessons we will ever learn are from our mistakes and failures.

Defeat. What is it? Nothing but a little education, nothing but the first step to something better. The only people who never fail are those who never, never try.

Mark Twain once told the story of a cat who one day jumped up on a hot stove and burned his tummy. That cat never again jumped up on a hot stove—but that cat never jumped up on a cold stove, either! Very often, the value of experience is overrated . . . and it can even be harmful if it prevents you from trying again once you've been bruised. There is a wonderful old Scandinavian saying, "The north wind made the Vikings." The north wind can do wonders for you, also.

Remember that even the most successful lives contain chapters of failure, just as any good novel does, but how the book ends depends on us. We are the authors of our years, and our failures and defeats are only steps to something better. Back in 1974, when Hank Aaron was approaching Babe Ruth's all-time home-run record, I phoned his ball club, the Atlanta Braves, one morning. I was finally put through to their public-relations department, and posed my question: "I know that Hank has seven-hundred-ten home runs and needs only five more to break Ruth's record, but I was wondering—how many lifetime strikeouts does he have?"

"Strikeouts, sir?" the young man on the line asked hesitantly.

"Yes, how many strikeouts?"

"I'm afraid I'll have to put you on hold while I check that one, sir."

He did, and it was several minutes before he came back on the line. "Mr. Mandino, as of last night, Hank has seven-hundred-ten home runs, and as you know, he needs only five more to break Babe Ruth's all-time home-run record . . ."

"Yes, I know . . ."

". . . and . . . lifetime, he has twelve-hundred-sixty-two strikeouts."

I thanked him, hung up, and then sat there pondering the figure I had just heard. What a great example to use in the future whenever I was trying to make the point about never letting past failures prevent you from trying again. Here was the greatest home-run hitter who has ever lived . . . and even he, even Hank Aaron, had to strike out almost *twice* for every time he hit one out of the park! Yes, life is a game, with rules that must be followed in order to triumph, but you don't have to hit a home run every time you come to bat in order to be a success in this world. Ask Hank.

RULE THREE
. . . for a Better Way to Live

Whenever you make a mistake or get knocked down by life, don't look back at it too long. Mistakes are life's way of teaching you. Your capacity for occasional blunders is inseparable from your capacity to reach your goals. No one wins them all, and your failures, when they happen, are just part of your growth. Shake off your blunders. How will you know your limits without an occasional failure? Never quit. Your turn will come.

IV

RULE FOUR

. . . for a Better Way to Live

Always reward your long hours of labor and toil in the very best way, surrounded by your family. Nurture their love carefully, remembering that your children need models, not critics, and your own progress will hasten when you constantly strive to present your best side to your children. And even if you have failed at all else in the eyes of the world, if you have a loving family, you are a success.

I am frequently being asked about my children, now grown, and how we raised them, as if, because of the books I have written, we must have some special magic formula guaranteed to succeed at everything . . . even producing bright, well-adjusted, happy citizens of tomorrow. Never forgetting that the "other Og Mandino," many years ago, lost his first family because of his inconsideration and neglect, I always give the same answer now. . . .

The best thing we can do for our children is to consciously work at being role models for them.

Teach them by your example, and they'll remember and even try to imitate. Talk to them one way and then act contrary to your words, and you've lost a kid. Other than guiding them by example, there isn't much we can do for them except *to be around to pick them up whenever they fall*. That's not asking too much, is it?

On this wall, facing my desk, is a brief poem wrought in calligraphy on white parchment and framed. Under the words "Author Unknown," I pasted, right after he was born, a small photo of Matt. You may want to bend this page down for future readings:

To Any Little Boy's Father

There are little eyes upon you, and
they're watching night and day,
There are little ears that quickly take
in everything you say,
There are little hands all eager to do
everything you do,
And a little boy who's dreaming of the
day he'll be like you.

You're the little fellow's idol, you're
the wisest of the wise,
In his little mind, about you no
suspicions ever rise.
He believes in you devoutly, holds that
all you say and do,
He will say and do in your way, when he's
grown up, just like you.

There's a wide-eyed little fellow who
believes you're always right,

And his ears are always open and he
watches day and night,
You are setting an example every day in
all you do,
For the little boy who's waiting to grow
up and be like you.

Several years ago, just prior to my hitting the
road for a long promotional tour for one of my
books, I had gone through the terrible agony of
helping our youngest son pack his things before
standing outside the front door, with his mother,
waving to him as he drove off to begin his own life
in an Arizona State University dormitory.

After he had gone, I remember walking down
the hall and sitting in the dark, in his room,
praying that Bette and I had provided Matt, and
our oldest son, Dana, with the guidance they
would need to deal with the many adversities of
life they were certain to face.

My promotional tour went well until I found
myself doing a morning talk show on a Los Angeles radio station. The other guest with me on this
live show was a very famous woman novelist who
shall remain nameless. Somehow the discussion
had drifted around to our families, and especially
our children.

The lady novelist quickly seized command of
the microphone and began a long and nasty dia-
tribe against her two teenage boys. She admitted
that she couldn't handle them, their father was no
help because he was never home, and these kids
were driving her "bonkers." They were never on
time for meals, their rooms were always a mess,
and they both played their stereo sets so loud,
with different stations, of course, that the noise

was also driving her "bonkers." After hearing that ugly word perhaps a dozen times while this celebrated author put down her children before a rather large listening audience, I finally lost my cool and interrupted. Couldn't help it.

"You know," I said, "the day is going to come when you're going to walk down that hallway, at home, and pass two very empty and quiet rooms . . . and then you're going to ask yourself, 'Where did they go?' Why don't you go home, right after this show, hug your boys, and just tell them you love them?"

RULE FOUR
. . . for a Better Way to Live

Always reward your long hours of labor and toil in the very best way, surrounded by your family. Nurture their love carefully, remembering that your children need models, not critics, and your own progress will hasten when you constantly strive to present your best side to your children. And even if you have failed at all else in the eyes of the world, if you have a loving family, you are a success.

V

```
RULE FIVE . . . for a Better Way to Live

Build this day on a foundation of pleasant
thoughts. Never fret at any imperfections
that you fear may impede your progress.
Remind yourself, as often as necessary, that
you are a creature of God and have the
power to achieve any dream by lifting up
your thoughts. You can fly when you decide
that you can. Never consider defeat again.
Let the vision in your heart be in your life's
blueprint. Smile!
```

Wise men, since the beginning of time, have been telling us that all we achieve, or fail to achieve, is the direct result of how we think—about our abilities, our courage, and our potential.

James Allen told us that good thoughts bear good fruit, bad thoughts bad fruit.

That wise old Roman Marcus Aurelius told us that our life is what our thoughts make it. Good or bad. Miserable or joyous. Triumphant or hopeless.

Buddha said it even more forcefully. "All that we are is the result of what we have thought. The mind is everything. What we think, we become."

No matter what you choose to call it, positive thoughts produce, negative thoughts hamper and destroy.

If you believe those very wise men, then you know that if you put yourself and your talents down, you are doomed to failure. If you disparage your ability or your background or your knowledge, the world will quickly go along with your evaluation, and you will face a sorry future that you don't deserve. Enough! No more negatives, in your thinking or your actions. Hear me out. *You just don't know how good you are!* Yes, you, sitting there and feeling sorry for yourself . . . you're so much like a duck we have out in our backyard.

Back when Matt was in junior high school, he came home one afternoon carrying a shoe box, with holes punched in its cover. My worst fears proved true when the cover came off. Inside was a frisky and noisy tiny yellow duckling. They had hatched the little guy in my son's biology class, nursed him for several weeks, and then had a lottery drawing and my kid won the duck—which both Bette and I agreed was just what we needed.

A reluctant father and his eager son went to the lumber company, bought some wooden planks, and over in the corner of our fenced-in yard, Matt built a great-looking duck house, which he painted white. Then, over the arched entrance, he hand-lettered, in red, DISCO. Disco duck! Next we purchased a roll of eighteen-inch chicken wire at the hardware store, and erected a corral of sorts around the hut so our new family member wouldn't go wandering off and get lost.

We've now had Disco for over a dozen years. He (she?) has grown into a very large and beautiful specimen, and of course, since Matt is now married and living elsewhere, I'm sure you can guess who takes care of the beast.

One of the mistakes we made, in the entire Disco affair, was building his little residence and play yard right outside our bedroom. Lately, Disco has been rising before the sun and quacking, with very few pauses, throughout the entire day. Loudly! Since he had never acted that way before, except to frighten away the neighbor's cat, both Bette and I have decided that there is something truly bothering Disco. He just is not happy anymore. Either the food I'm giving him is distasteful, or perhaps I don't change the water in his little wading pool often enough, or maybe the straw in his hut is damp and needs changing or removal. Who knows? I've tried everything to make him feel secure and contented once more, but he still sounds off, raucously and constantly.

Disco, you see, does indeed have a problem, and I'll wager it's the same one you have. Yes, you! Neither Disco nor you have a proper sense of self-worth. Disco has no idea that if he is unhappy with the conditions in his life, he can do more than just feel sorry for himself; he has the power to *change* those conditions instead of just complaining about them.

If Disco truly wants to change the conditions in his life, he can do so whenever he chooses. Simple. All he has to do is raise his pretty wings, flap them up and down . . . and leave. But you see, poor Disco doesn't know how good he is. He doesn't know that he can fly . . . and *neither do you*!

RULE FIVE . . . for a Better Way to Live

Build this day on a foundation of pleasant thoughts. Never fret at any imperfections that you fear may impede your progress. Remind yourself, as often as necessary, that you are a creature of God and have the power to achieve any dream by lifting up your thoughts. You can fly when you decide that you can. Never consider defeat again. Let the vision in your heart be in your life's blueprint. Smile!

VI

RULE SIX . . . for a Better Way to Live

Let your actions always speak for you, but be forever on guard against the terrible traps of false pride and conceit that can halt your progress. The next time you are tempted to boast, just place your fist in a full pail of water, and when you remove it, the hole remaining will give you a correct measure of your importance.

None of us are ever deceived by another as much as we deceive ourselves. A dangerous obstacle to our continued progress is the terrible screen of smug conceit that is liable to blind our forward progress after we have tasted a little success. True, we may have worked very hard and applied all our talents and efforts to move forward, and that is really what you and I being together is all about; however, it is easy to fall into the trap of believing, after a few victories, that you possess some special and unique qualities, and if you reflect that attitude in your behavior toward others, it can seriously hurt your progress. Nothing, in fact, can harm you more than arrogance and conceit begging to be slapped down.

We are all God's creatures, but if we could only see how small a vacancy our death would leave on this earth, we would think less of the space we're occupying and more about helping others.

I am constantly waging my own personal battle against the temptation of false pride. When one writes a new book every two years, as I do, and then tours the nation to discuss it on radio and television and with the press, not to mention delivering scores of keynote speeches each year, it is easy to fall into that trap of beginning to believe all the nice things the media say and write—not to mention being spoiled by all the attention, the chauffeur-driven limousines, and the autograph parties.

I'll never forget the day that God decided to reduce my head size several notches, which I undoubtedly deserved at the time. I was in my hotel room, waiting for the knock on the door that would signal it was time for me to make my appearance in the ballroom below, where I was to keynote a large national convention of several thousand. When the company's messenger, an elderly man, finally arrived, I slipped on my jacket and followed him down the hall to the elevator.

The lobby was noisy and crowded, and we had not traveled very far when I felt a firm tap on my shoulder and turned to see a wide-eyed young man, complete with his company name badge attached to his jacket pocket, clutching a paper shopping bag and pointing at my face. "Are you Og Mandino?" he asked breathlessly.

I nodded and kept walking.

"Can you spare a minute, sir?" he implored,

moving toward a small table against a window that was away from the flow of traffic. I glanced at my frowning guide, who finally nodded reluctantly.

"Sir," the young man exhaled as he placed the shopping bag on the table, "I want you to know that my wife is an Og Mandino nut. I swear that she has read everything you have ever written. She teaches back in our small hometown, and so there was no way she could come with me to this convention and she's heartbroken. She wanted to hear you so badly."

"I'm sorry."

"Well, sir, I thought I'd do something special for Louise, and I reckon I've been in every bookstore for fifty miles around our town and I've managed to find five of your books in hard cover. Please . . . please . . . would you do me the great honor of autographing these books for my lady? I want to give them to her for her birthday, next Thursday."

"I'd be happy to," I said, removing my pen from the inside pocket of my jacket and writing, in all five books, *To Louise, with love, Happy Birthday, Og Mandino*.

When I had finished, the young man gently returned all the books to his shopping bag, gave me a nervous and hasty hug, thanked me, and turned away . . . and I forgot to keep my mouth shut, but I'm glad I did forget.

He was about ten feet away when I yelled after him, "Say, is this going to be a surprise for Louise!"

He turned, with a sheepish smile extending from ear to ear, and yelled back, "It certainly will be, sir—she's expecting a new Toyota Corolla!"

RULE SIX . . . for a Better Way to Live

Let your actions always speak for you, but be forever on guard against the terrible traps of false pride and conceit that can halt your progress. The next time you are tempted to boast, just place your fist in a full pail of water, and when you remove it, the hole remaining will give you a correct measure of your importance.

VII

RULE SEVEN
. . . for a Better Way to Live

Each day is a special gift from God, and
while life may not always be fair, you must
never allow the pains, hurdles, and handicaps of the moment to poison your attitude
and plans for yourself and your future. You
can never win when you wear the ugly cloak
of self-pity, and the sour sound of whining
will certainly frighten away any opportunity
for success. Never again. There is a better
way.

Life isn't fair . . . and probably never will
be. There may be times when you do most of the
work and yet someone else gets the credit. You
may work twice as hard as your neighbor, and you
know you're twice as smart . . . and yet you earn
only half the money that he or she does.

There are many times when life deals us a bad
hand. How do you play the bad hands when *you*
get one? Do you hang on, refusing to give up, even
though you have no guarantee you'll succeed . . .
or do you whine and pity yourself because you
are certain that your troubles and problems are

far more terrible than anyone else's misfortunes? Poor baby!

Almost two decades ago, I received a tiny yellow card with a poem on it, printed in green, from Wilton Hall, who was publisher of *Quote Magazine* in Anderson, South Carolina. The poem has had a special place in my life through all these many years. I not only share it, during my speech, with all my audiences, but I keep it handy for my own well-being. Whenever things aren't going quite the way I planned or the day gets off on the wrong foot or I begin to feel a little irritated with others and maybe a little sorry for myself, I pull out my poem, read it, and then get on with my life, gratefully, pausing only long enough to look up into the heavens to say, "Thank you . . ."

Yes, lean over and let me give you the original dog-eared copy. It's a treasure, and I'll bet that you, too, like me, will come back to it often in the future, as well as sharing it with your friends.

Lord, Forgive Me When I Whine!

Today, upon a bus, I saw a lovely girl with golden hair, I envied her . . . she seemed so gay . . . and wished I were as fair. When suddenly she rose to leave, I saw her hobble down the aisle; She had one leg and wore a crutch; But as she passed . . . a smile! Oh, God forgive me when I whine, I have two legs. The world is mine!

I stopped to buy some candy. The lad who sold it had such charm. I talked with him. He seemed so glad. If I were late 'twould do no harm. And as I left he said to me, "I thank you. You have been so kind. It's nice to talk with folks like you. You see," he said, "I'm blind." Oh, God, forgive me when I whine, I have two eyes. The world is mine.

Later, while walking down the street, I saw a child with eyes of blue. He stood and watched the others play. He did not know what to do. I stopped a moment, then I said, "Why don't you join the others, dear?" He looked ahead without a word, and then I knew he could not hear. Oh, God forgive me when I whine. I have two ears. The world is mine.

With feet to take me where I'd go, with eyes to see the sunset's glow, With ears to hear what I would know . . . Oh, God forgive me when I whine. I'm blessed indeed. The world is mine.

Author Unknown

RULE SEVEN
. . . for a Better Way to Live

Each day is a special gift from God, and while life may not always be fair, you must never allow the pains, hurdles, and handicaps of the moment to poison your attitude and plans for yourself and your future. You can never win when you wear the ugly cloak of self-pity, and the sour sound of whining will certainly frighten away any opportunity for success. Never again. There is a better way.

VIII

RULE EIGHT
. . . for a Better Way to Live

Never again clutter your days or nights with
so many menial and unimportant things that
you have no time to accept a real challenge
when it comes along. This applies to play as
well as work. A day merely survived is no
cause for celebration. You are not here to
fritter away your precious hours when you
have the ability to accomplish so much by
making a slight change in your routine. No
more busywork. No more hiding from success. Leave time, leave space, to grow.
Now. Now! Not tomorrow!

You may know this type of person. You may
even be one. If you are, I'm glad you've come to
me. He or she is always busy, always has more
projects and meetings and errands than can be
handled, and there is always frantic scurrying
from place to place to try—just to try—to stay
ahead of things. What these type of people are
involved in is an unconscious but very effective
effort to *avoid* success. Oh, they're busy alright—
doing every possible insignificant chore and task

they can find so that if they are ever presented with a real challenge, something that could truly make a great difference in their lives and their welfare, it is always easy for them to respond that they're sorry but they're just too *busy* right now to take on any more.

Sound familiar? I hope that you haven't been unconsciously working hard at failing by keeping yourself involved in "busywork" that won't do anything for you but keep you in that long rut. If it's any consolation, you've got plenty of company. It takes just as much energy to fail, you know, as it does to succeed, and that's why we have so many active, busy people who cannot understand why nothing is happening in their lives.

If you happen to think you may be in that category, maybe you're doing what you're doing because someone pushed your "kill switch" years ago. Yes, your "kill switch!" I was going to do a whole book on this, years ago, but this is the first time I've discussed it in print.

Once I purchased a very expensive convertible automobile, and of course the dealer persuaded me that I should not take that priceless vehicle on the street and park it in any public lot before having a burglar alarm installed that would erupt in a loud and piercing siren if anyone ever tried to break in, jump-start my jewel, and drive it away. Of course, I agreed.

One morning, late for an appointment, I dashed out to my garage, inserted the key in the ignition, turned it . . . but nothing happened. Not even a moan. Nothing. Battery stone-dead? Doubtful. I turned on the radio. It played, loudly. I inserted a cassette in the tape player. Ella Fitzgerald and her "Mack the Knife." Great fidelity. I turned on the windshield wipers. Two sprays of water spurted from hidden openings, and the wipers flapped back and forth in perfect synchrony. Frustrated and angry, I stormed back into the house and called my friendly auto salesperson.

"We installed a burglar alarm in that baby, didn't we, Og?"

"Three hundred bucks' worth!"

"Then you probably have accidentally tripped the 'kill switch.'"

"The 'kill switch'?"

"Yes, it's a feature of the more sophisticated burglar-alarm systems. Didn't they explain it to you when they installed the unit?"

I was getting angrier by the moment. "I would certainly have remembered anybody talking about putting a 'kill switch' in my car. What is it and where is it?"

"It's part of the burglar alarm. After you leave the auto and lock it, you then turn another key in that little slot that was installed in your fender, right? That activates the alarm so that if anyone tries to jimmy open any door or breaks one of the windows, the alarm is triggered."

"Right."

"Well, the 'kill switch' is an additional level of protection. Somewhere inside the car, usually under the dash or beneath the rug, another small switch was installed. If you push that, prior to your leaving the car, and then lock the door and turn on your alarm, you are truly protected against car theft. Even if someone breaks in and they're foolish enough to try to jump-start the car while the alarm is sounding, they will fail, because once you've turned on the 'kill switch,' it cuts off all power going from the battery to the ignition. The car cannot be moved."

I returned to the garage, but I could not locate my "kill switch," and within an hour the sales rep was at the house. Of course, he found it almost immediately, under the front carpet on the driver's side. Yes, the switch had been tripped. I had probably accidentally nudged it with my foot, but I couldn't remain angry, even with myself, since the priceless analogy that incident provided me with, which related to so many human beings I knew, has been invaluable to me when I'm trying to convince someone that he or she is wasting too much time on "busy" but inconsequential work.

You see, my automobile really had acted quite normal when I first turned the key in the ignition. Its lights went on, its radio played, its windshield wipers zapped back and forth. Busy, busy car. Like so many people I know. Only one problem. The machine was unable to move forward even a single inch despite all its activity, because I had tripped its "kill switch."

All of us have our own "kill switches." Perhaps when we were young, someone, even a parent or another respected adult, or a spouse in later years, might have told us one day, in a fit of anger, that we would never amount to much. Zap! That did it! Unknowingly, and unthinking, they pushed our switch, and we've been spending all these years working very hard to make their prophecy come true, without even understanding the motivation for our actions. We're "busy" alright, but like my car, we're not going anywhere. And we don't understand why. How sad.

A BETTER WAY TO LIVE

Reach down and turn off that "kill switch" now that you know you have one. "Busywork" is out. Stop hiding behind all those petty chores. There's a better way to live.

RULE EIGHT
. . . for a Better Way to Live

Never again clutter your days or nights with so many menial and unimportant things that you have no time to accept a real challenge when it comes along. This applies to play as well as work. A day merely survived is no cause for celebration. You are not here to fritter away your precious hours when you have the ability to accomplish so much by making a slight change in your routine. No more busywork. No more hiding from success. Leave time, leave space, to grow. Now. Now! Not tomorrow!

IX

RULE NINE . . . for a Better Way to Live

Live this day as if it will be your last. Remember that you will only find "tomorrow" on the calendars of fools. Forget yesterday's defeats, and ignore the problems of tomorrow. This is it. Doomsday. All you have. Make it the best day of your year. The saddest words you can ever utter are, "If I had my life to live over again . . ." Take the baton, now. Run with it! This is your day!

Most failures always act as if they had a thousand years to live. Why? Simply because they have no confidence that they can handle the challenges of today. And how do they avoid ever having to test their potential? A hundred different ways. Some of them drink too much, or party to excess. Many of them sleep two or three hours a night more than they need. Others spend endless hours over crossword puzzles or jigsaw puzzles or squatting in front of that television set.

"Don't worry," they will always assure you. "Everything will be taken care of . . . tomorrow." Tomorrow? I've been around this old planet for a lot of years, and in that time I've seen thousands of calendars, but never . . . never have I seen one with a "tomorrow" on it.

Never treat time as if you had an unlimited supply. You have no contract with life. If yesterday is already a canceled check, then tomorrow is just a promissory note. Today is all you have in the way of cash, and if you don't spend it wisely, you have only yourself to blame. Father Time makes no round trips for our benefit.

None of us have learned very much until we train ourselves to treat every day as a separate life. Those fortunate millions of individuals who have been saved by Alcoholics Anonymous know full well the power in the words "a day at a time." Robert Louis Stevenson once wrote, "Anyone can carry his or her burden, however hard, until nightfall. Anyone can do his work, however hard, for one day. Anyone can live sweetly, patiently, lovingly, purely, till the sun goes down. And this is all that life really means."

As difficult as it may be, you can handle today's load, one task at a time, and make progress toward your goals. It is only when you spend countless and tearful hours reliving your past mistakes, or worrying about the terrible things that might happen tomorrow, that you let this precious day, which is all you have, slip away.

Today is your day, the only day you have, that day in which you can show the world that you can make a contribution that matters. What your part may signify in the great whole of life you may never understand, but you are still here to play it, and now is your time. No matter how crowded the hours, remember that they still can only enter your life just one moment at a time. You can handle any moment, no matter how tough, when it comes at you in single file.

When you have finished your day, be done with it. Never save any of your load to carry on the morrow. You have done your best, and if some blunders and errors have crept in, forget them. Live this day, and every day, as if it all may end at sunset, and when your head hits that pillow, rest, knowing that you have done your best.

RULE NINE . . . for a Better Way to Live

Live this day as if it will be your last. Remember that you will only find "tomorrow" on the calendars of fools. Forget yesterday's defeats, and ignore the problems of tomorrow. This is it. Doomsday. All you have. Make it the best day of your year. The saddest words you can ever utter are, "If I had my life to live over again . . ." Take the baton, now. Run with it! This is your day!

X

RULE TEN . . . for a Better Way to Live

Beginning today, treat everyone you meet, friend or foe, loved one or stranger, as if they were going to be dead at midnight. Extend to each person, no matter how trivial the contact, all the care and kindness and understanding and love that you can muster, and do it with no thought of any reward. Your life will never be the same again.

Like the rules in any game, all of the rules of life are related to each other. Follow the guidance of one rule and it will lead you to the next, and the next, but now you're beginning to play the game of life as it should be played.

To live every day as if it's the only one you will ever have is indeed one of the supreme principles of a happy and successful existence. But here is a companion rule that is just as powerful and productive, and yet, unlike the other, is known to very few people.

While you are living each day as if it's the only one you'll ever have, begin treating *everyone* you meet—your fam   your neighbors, your coworkers, strangers, customers, even enemies, if you have any—as if you knew a deep, dark secret about each of them. The secret: that they, too, are living their last day on this earth, and will be dead by midnight!

Now, how do you suppose you would treat everyone you meet today, if you knew that they would be gone forever at day's end? You know how. With more consideration and care and tenderness and love than you ever have before. And how do you suppose they would react to your kindness? Of course. With more consideration and kindness and cooperation and love than you have ever experienced from others in the past. Continue doing the same, day after day, and what do you suppose your future would be like, if you filled it with that kind of unselfish love? You're smiling already. You know the answer.

Years ago, whenever authors were sent out on a publicity tour to promote their books on radio, television, and with the press, they were pretty much on their own compared to today, when they are literally taken by the hand from city to city and interview to interview by paid publishers' representatives in each city. In those "old days" our publishers mailed us airline tickets plus hotel reservations and a schedule of our appearances in each city. It was then the author's responsibility to get to airports and hotels and to take cabs from interview to interview. If one had seven or eight commitments in a day, which was not uncommon, and the interviews were spread out in time and distance, such as in Los Angeles, it became a supreme challenge of one's endurance and agility just getting from one appointment to the next, on time.

This memorable day happened in Nashville several years ago while I was on tour. A young black cabbie drove me from my hotel out into the suburbs for an appearance on *The Noon Show* on WSM-TV. Since the ride took some time, we began to converse, and the driver, whose name, I learned, was Raymond Bright, seemed fascinated by the fact that his fare was going to be on television.

My elaborate printed schedule informed me that this program was live, with a studio audience, and was similar in format to *The Tonight Show,* even to having its own band and perhaps a singer or two. As we pulled up to the lovely building, my cabbie said loudly, "This here is the best darn station in Nashville!"

Perhaps it was because the rule of treating others with love and care, as if they were going to be dead at midnight, was still fresh in my mind since I had talked about it at length on several programs the day before, but anyway, as I was paying Ray, I asked impulsively, "Have you ever seen them put on a television show?"

"No, sir."

"Well . . . if you've got an hour or so, and it's okay if you charge me for your waiting, why don't you come on in with me and watch me make a fool of myself."

His eyes opened wide. "You mean it?"

"Sure, and then when it's over, you can drive me back downtown to the Cokesbury bookstore, where I'm autographing books at one-thirty."

Raymond leaped back into his cab, turned the yellow flag on his meter up, meaning he wasn't charging me at all, and jumped out. Inside the station, I introduced my new friend to a surprised

Teddy Bart, the host of the show, and Elaine Ganick, the producer, and they led us both into the bright studio where the band was already tuning up. Ray was ushered to a prime seat, down front, and while I went off to confer with Teddy and Elaine on what we were going to talk about, he watched in awe as the band ran through their numbers while the television cameras and boom mikes swept back and forth in final rehearsal.

When the show was over, we raced downtown to the bookstore. After that, I told Ray that I was starved, and he took me to lunch in what he called "my part of town," and although I was the only white person in the place, the hamburgers were the best I had ever eaten. When it came time to pay, I reached for my wallet, but a strong arm restrained me. Ray was paying, and that was all there was to it. No argument. He drove me to two more radio shows, waited for me, drove me back to my hotel so that I could check out, and then hauled me to the airport.

On the way, as I was beginning to doze in the backseat, I heard his deep voice. "Mr. Og (by then he was calling me what the hosts on the radio shows had been calling me earlier) . . . Mr. Og, I ain't never gonna forget this day as long as I live."

"Why, Ray?"

"Because today, for the first time in my life, I feel important."

All the way to the airport, every now and then I would see those big brown eyes staring at me in his rearview mirror and hear him repeating, again and again, "You made me feel important!"

At the airport Ray leaped from the cab and brought my luggage to the check-in station. Then I paid him, and he stepped close to me and hugged me—shocking a few onlookers—and there were huge tears rolling down his cheeks.

"I love you, Mr. Og," he mumbled.

"And I love you too, Ray," I replied hoarsely.

Dead at midnight. A vision preceding a new way to treat everyone you meet. It's really easy to do, and what you'll receive in return can change your life forever. Try it!

RULE TEN . . . for a Better Way to Live

Beginning today, treat everyone you meet, friend or foe, loved one or stranger, as if they were going to be dead at midnight. Extend to each person, no matter how trivial the contact, all the care and kindness and understanding and love that you can muster, and do it with no thought of any reward. Your life will never be the same again.

XI

RULE ELEVEN
. . . for a Better Way to Live

Laugh at yourself and at life. Not in the spirit of derision or whining self-pity, but as a remedy, a miracle drug, that will ease your pain, cure your depression, and help you to put in perspective that seemingly terrible defeat of the moment. Banish tension and concern and worry with laughter at your predicaments, thus freeing your mind to think clearly toward the solution that is certain to come. Never take yourself too seriously.

The most utterly desolate of days are those that have not heard the sound of your laughter. A good laugh is sunshine in any house, so never let a day pass without some outward expression of your happy side, even when you're struggling with chaos. Every time you smile, and more so when you laugh, you add precious moments to your life.

Man is the only creature endowed with the power of laughter, and perhaps is the only creature that deserves to be laughed at. The finest of all laughter, however, is that of the person who has enough self-confidence to laugh at himself. This shows the rare ability to look at oneself objectively, and if you can do that, all your worries will shrink in size.

Yes, there are rules in order to play this difficult game of life effectively, but you must never forget that it's still a *game*—a game that none of us should ever take too seriously. If we don't manage to squeeze a little joy from this day, what is there? Laughing at myself, and certainly not taking myself too seriously, is a rule of the game that I have to keep learning and relearning. Whenever I begin to act a little too professorial or pompous or fall into the "famous author" role, God always sets me up for another deserved tumble to straighten me out . . . until the next time.

I had just spent several days visiting radio and television stations in the Atlanta area, and I was now being driven, in a black limo, to autograph books in a shopping mall nearly two hours from the city. My schedule indicated that on the way I was to visit a small Christian radio station, where I would do thirty minutes on live radio with a gentleman known as "Reverend John."

Eventually, we pulled up in front of a small white cottage with its white paint beginning to peel. My driver turned, half-apologetically, and said, "This is it, sir. The radio station."

Before I had reached the top step, the front door flew open, and there stood Reverend John. Now I knew it was my man because he had "Reverend John" elaborately stitched in red above the breast pocket of his white jumpsuit.

"Welcome to our humble station, sir!" he exclaimed as he embraced me. "This is such an honor."

We passed through what had once probably been a living room but was now cluttered with electronic equipment and piles of records and tapes. I could hear psalms being played as the reverend led me to his "studio" in the rear.

"We'll be going on in just a few minutes," my host said. "Have a seat there, and make yourself comfortable."

Reverend John was nodding toward an unpainted table on which a microphone was perched precariously, attached to the boards by several nails. I slid myself onto the rough bench, wondering if my publishers, back in their plush Fifth Avenue offices, had any idea what they put their authors through. Then, to my great surprise, Reverend John lowered himself down alongside me on the bench, and it suddenly dawned on me that the microphone on the table was the *only* microphone, and we were going to share it. Quite a change after spending days in all the glitz and glitter and glass of the Atlanta stations. But, I reassured myself, I can take anything for thirty minutes.

On that tour the book I was promoting was *The Christ Commission,* and unlike so many interviewers, who never read your book before the interview, Reverend John had not only read the book but had prepared a long list of very perceptive questions, on a legal pad, which he constantly referred to once we went on the air.

I was truly enjoying our discussion when, approximately halfway through the interview, a telephone rang, loudly, in the other room. Of course, this "studio" was not soundproof, as most are, so that the rude ringing, coming in the middle of my response to a question, knocked me completely off balance, and I almost lost my train of thought as I fumbled to regain my composure.

The damnable phone continued to ring and ring. Finally, an annoyed Reverend John glanced at his legal pad, asked me the next question on his list, and then, before my horrified eyes, turned, threw a leg over the bench, stood, and vanished into the other room, presumably to answer the phone. Now I'm talking to an empty bench—and a live microphone—and I spoke . . . very . . . slowly, stalling, not knowing what I would do if I completed my response and my friend had not returned.

Finally, I had exhausted that subject, and Reverend John was nowhere. And then, for once in my life, I did something bright. I reached over and slid his legal pad around in front of me, ran my finger down his list of questions, found the next one, and said, "Reverend John, I imagine you're wondering where I got the idea for *The Christ Commission?*"

. . . and for the next fourteen minutes, I interviewed myself!

Finally, I felt a tap on my shoulder. I had become so engrossed with my double role of interviewer and interviewee that I hadn't even noticed that my host had returned. He pointed to the huge clock on the wall, leaned over, and said into our microphone, "Mr. Mandino, it was a great honor to have you with us today. I wish you great success with this marvelous book, and a safe trip for the remainder of your tour. God bless."

With that, he hit a button, and "Nearer My God to Thee" went out over the airwaves while I sat back, wiping my brow. That's when I was reminded, once again, of that very important rule of life telling us to laugh at ourselves. Reverend John was waving a file card before my eyes and looking pleased with himself.

"Mr. Mandino, I'm so sorry to have put you through that ordeal, but you handled it masterfully. That phone call was from my eighty-year-old mother in San Diego, and the last time we spoke, she promised that the next time she phoned, she would give me our old family recipe for carrot cake."

Laugh at the world. Most important, laugh at yourself. If laughter could be dispensed at your favorite drugstore, your family doctor would have you taking some every day. It's a much better way to live.

RULE ELEVEN
. . . for a Better Way to Live

Laugh at yourself and at life. Not in the spirit of derision or whining self-pity, but as a remedy, a miracle drug, that will ease your pain, cure your depression, and help you to put in perspective that seemingly terrible defeat of the moment. Banish tension and concern and worry with laughter at your predicaments, thus freeing your mind to think clearly toward the solution that is certain to come. Never take yourself too seriously.

XII

RULE TWELVE
. . . for a better Way to Live

Never neglect the little things. Never skimp on that extra effort, that additional few minutes, that soft word of praise or thanks, that delivery of the very best that you can do. It does not matter what others think, it is of prime importance, however, what you think about you. You can never do your best, which should always be your trademark, if you are cutting corners and shirking responsibilities. You are special. Act it. Never neglect the little things!

Teacher, student, factory worker, salesperson, executive, parent, coach, athlete, cab driver, elevator operator, doctor, lawyer—whatever challenges you accept in this life, whatever tasks you must perform for your daily bread . . . never, never neglect the little things.

We are indeed living in an age that seems to be traveling faster than the speed of light, and in our hurry-up world it is easy to fall into that habit of taking shortcuts, of skipping some of our duties, when we think we can get away with it. We forget the lessons of history and the warnings of wise men. To neglect the little things, in whatever you are doing, can be disastrous.

Edison lost a valuable patent because he had carelessly misplaced a single decimal point. Robert DeVincenzo lost a Masters Tournament because he had signed, without taking the time to check, his scorecard, which contained an incorrect score. And I'm sure you once could recite Benjamin Franklin's wise words, "For want of a nail the shoe was lost; for want of a shoe the horse was lost; for want of a horse the rider was lost and for want of a rider the battle was lost."

It is everyone's dream, of course, to find work to do in this world that one loves to do so much that one would be willing to do it for nothing. Unfortunately, this doesn't happen to very many, and so most of us, growing bored with our life's task, gradually ease off from doing our best, cutting corners whenever we can. Not to mention what this way of life will do to your image of yourself, little things that are ignored or carelessly handled can often lead to larger problems that are certain to impede your progress. You are a special creation of God. Never allow anything that originates with you, in deeds or materials or effort or kindness, to be less than your best. Only the failures and the mediocrities neglect the little things.

A potent example of this simple but powerful truth, this enduring rule of life, stands high above Liberty Island in New York Harbor. Should you ever be in New York City with an extra few hours to enjoy, take one of the several helicopter cruises that depart from the foot of East Thirty-fourth Street on the East River. When you finally approach the lovely Statue of Liberty, standing proudly in the harbor, pay special attention.

Lady Liberty's steel-frame-supported copper body stands 305 feet above sea level. As your helicopter circles closer, look down at the top of Liberty's head and note how every strand of hair has been painstakingly formed in careful and minute detail, just as is every other area of her gown and body. That delicate metallic coiffure on the top of her head undoubtedly required many additional weeks at Auguste Bartholdi's shop in Paris, weeks that the great sculptor could have saved, because so far as he knew, *no one* would ever see the top of Liberty's head!

The statue was dedicated on October 28, 1886, by President Grover Cleveland. There were no airplanes in 1886! The Wright Brothers would not even get their first primitive contraption off the ground at Kitty Hawk until seventeen years later! Bartholdi was well aware that only a few brave sea gulls would probably ever look down on the statue from above, and certainly no one would ever know if the strands of hair had not been meticulously shaped and polished. And yet, the master artisan took no shortcuts. Every strand of hair, every curl, is in place!

RULE TWELVE
. . . for a Better Way to Live

Never neglect the little things. Never skimp on that extra effort, that additional few minutes, that soft word of praise or thanks, that delivery of the very best that you can do. It does not matter what others think, it is of prime importance, however, what you think about you. You can never do your best, which should always be your trademark, if you are cutting corners and shirking responsibilities. You are special. Act it. Never neglect the little things!

XIII

RULE THIRTEEN
. . . for a Better Way to Live

Welcome every morning with a smile. Look on the new day as another special gift from your Creator, another golden opportunity to complete what you were unable to finish yesterday. Be a self-starter. Let your first hour set the theme of success and positive action that is certain to echo through your entire day. Today will never happen again. Don't waste it with a false start or no start at all. You were not born to fail.

Be a self-starter. Welcome the dawn of each new day with a smile, grateful to your Creator for another opportunity to improve on yesterday's performance. So many of us crawl, fearful, from our place of rest, dreading what the new day will bring, never realizing that how we act during those first few hours will stamp its imprint on the entire day, as well as prepare us for tomorrow and all the other tomorrows that follow.

How terrible to awake facing a day so bleak and painful and boring that all we have to look forward to is the merciful sleep that awaits us after the sun has set.

There is a better way to live. To confront each morning with hope shining in your eyes, to welcome the day with reverence for the opportunities it contains, to greet everyone you meet with laughter and love, to be gentle, kind, and courteous toward friend and foe, and to enjoy the satisfaction of work well done during precious hours that will never return—that is the way to leave your footprints.

Above all, greet the morning with a smile. Easy enough? Now, if this simple act is a problem for you, if you awake and feel you have nothing to smile about, don't despair. Happens to all of us. There are many days when even the most positive of individuals would much prefer to remain in the solitude of their rooms rather than confront a world that sometimes can be hostile and uncaring. All of us have "down" days, even the most powerful world figures, superstar athletes, and corporation presidents. Everyone now and then awakes with the feeling that he would much rather hide his head under that fluffy pillow instead of inching along that choked freeway or making that first sales call or facing that nasty boss.

Now, the next morning that you awake feeling terrible about all the aggravation with little reward that lies ahead, here's the perfect prescription to send you out into the world with an attitude so positive that you cannot avoid having a great day. This simple trick or technique or whatever you want to call it has never failed, won't cost you a penny, and yet will do more for you than your orange juice, steak and eggs, coffee, or any motivational tape ever made—sending you out into the world with an attitude that is positive, powerful, productive and . . . *grateful*.

All you have to do to turn on the sunshine and turn up the music whenever you awake feeling sorry for yourself is just pick up your morning paper. Don't ever look on that front page in the early hours, or you will really want to crawl into that basement and hide. Instead, open your paper to the . . . *obituary page*!

On that page you will find a long list of names of people who would be absolutely delighted to change places with you, even with all your aggravations, doubts, fears, and problems! Try it whenever you're feeling low in the morning. You'll thank me.

Hear the birds singing now?

RULE THIRTEEN
. . . for a Better Way to Live

Welcome every morning with a smile. Look on the new day as another special gift from your Creator, another golden opportunity to complete what you were unable to finish yesterday. Be a self-starter. Let your first hour set the theme of success and positive action that is certain to echo through your entire day. Today will never happen again. Don't waste it with a false start or no start at all. You were not born to fail.

XIV

RULE FOURTEEN
. . . for a Better Way to Live

You will achieve your grand dream, a day at a time, so set goals for each day—not long and difficult projects, but chores that will take you, step by step, toward your rainbow. Write them down, if you must, but limit your list so that you won't have to drag today's undone matters into tomorrow. Remember that you cannot build your pyramid in twenty-four hours. Be patient. Never allow your day to become so cluttered that you neglect your most important goal—to do the best you can, enjoy this day, and rest satisfied with what you have accomplished.

Setting goals is easy. As with New Year's resolutions, any of us can jot down long lists of things we hope to accomplish in the future . . . but then we continue to live exactly as we have in the past.

Let's tackle that elusive but necessary project once more, and let me help you. First, a warning. Any goal that forces you to labor, day after day and year after year, so long and hard that you never have any time for yourself and those you love is not a goal but a sentence . . . a sentence to a lifetime of misery, no matter how much wealth and success you attain.

We often are told that "life is a journey." So-called motivational experts use the phrase incessantly, book jackets proclaim it, and you can hear it on scores of tapes: "Life is a journey!" Sounds so eloquent it must be true. Pipe-organ music, at the very least, should accompany such great wisdom.

What that silly phrase is telling you is that you must fight and struggle and work unending hours to get to the first plateau of success. But hold on, that's not enough. Life is a journey. So take a deep breath, ask those you love to get out of your way, and continue to toil and battle, days and nights, until eventually you arrive at your second plateau. Great! Now, you relax? Sorry. It's a journey, my friend, so take a deep breath and keep fighting and sweating and agonizing until you get to the next plateau and then the next.

And then, one day . . .

Tolstoy, the brilliant Russian novelist, left us a powerful allegory of how man has always failed at fulfilling goals that have little to do with our happiness and the enjoyment of the brief time we have on this earth. A peasant named Pakhom is certain that he will be a great success when he finally has as much land as is contained in the vast estates possessed by the most elite Russian noblemen. That is his goal. The day arrives when he receives an amazing offer—he will be awarded, at no cost, as much land as he himself can encircle by running from sunrise to sunset.

Pakhom sells all his worldly goods in order to move to the far-distant place where this generous offer has been made. After many hardships, he arrives, and arranges to capitalize on his great opportunity the next day.

At dawn, Pakhom begins to run at breakneck speed. Dashing into the bright morning sun, his goal fixed before his eyes, he races along in the blistering heat, looking neither to the left or right. All day, he continues his swift pace, stopping neither for food nor water nor rest, his estate growing larger with each stride. Finally, as the sun disappears beyond the desert and darkness envelops the land, Pakhom staggers to the finish line. Victory! His goal has been achieved. Success!

And then . . . with his final step, Pakhom drops dead from exhaustion. All the land he now needs . . . is six feet of earth.

Success is not a journey. This day, like all the others, is a special gift from God. Set goals so that you will fulfill your potential for the day, even by going the extra mile, but let some of your goals give you joy and smiles and peace. And plan those daily goals so that they are but steps along the path toward the great dreams you hold secretly in your heart. Give yourself every chance to succeed, and if you fail, fail trying.

Listen to that wise old Roman Seneca. "True happiness is to enjoy the present, without anxious dependence upon the future, not to amuse ourselves with either hopes or fears but to rest satisfied with what we have, which is sufficient, for he that is so wants nothing. The great blessings of mankind are within us and within our reach. A wise man is content with his lot, whatever it be, without wishing for what he has not."

Despite a long and illustrious career, rewarded by both worldly recognition and material goods, a great American comic recently admitted in an interview that he's never been secure with his success. He said, "I get the feeling, sometimes, that I'm going to wake up one morning and it's all going to be gone. Someone's going to say, 'That's it, fella, it's all over for you.'" And so, although past age sixty, this multitalented man continues to run, like Pakhom, making endless appearances in theaters, nightclubs, movies, and television. His fans are glad he does, but I wish he'd also stop and smell those roses now and then, before the petals all blow away.

We are all being swept along in the whirlpool of change, as Schopenhauer warned us, where a person, if he or she is to keep erect at all, must always be advancing and moving, like an acrobat on a rope. How sad. There is a better way to live.

RULE FOURTEEN
. . . for a Better Way to Live

You will achieve your grand dream, a day at a time, so set goals for each day—not long and difficult projects, but chores that will take you, step by step, toward your rainbow. Write them down, if you must, but limit your list so that you won't have to drag today's undone matters into tomorrow. Remember that you cannot build your pyramid in twenty-four hours. Be patient. Never allow your day to become so cluttered that you neglect your most important goal—to do the best you can, enjoy this day, and rest satisfied with what you have accomplished.

XV

RULE FIFTEEN
. . . for a Better Way to Live

Never allow anyone to rain on your parade
and thus cast a pall of gloom and defeat on
the entire day. Remember that no talent, no
self-denial, no brains, no character, are required to set up in the fault-finding business. Nothing external can have any power
over you unless you permit it. Your time is
too precious to be sacrificed in wasted days
combating the menial forces of hate, jealousy, and envy. Guard your fragile life carefully. Only God can shape a flower, but any
foolish child can pull it to pieces.

Life, Montaigne told us, is a tender thing, and
easily molested. There is always something that
can go wrong. Often, the slightest and smallest
mishaps are the most troubling, and as tiny letters
most tire our eyes, so do these little vexations
most disturb us and cloud our day, if we let them.

We humans are extremely fragile animals. We
can awake with a song on our lips and joyful
anticipation of the hours ahead in our hearts, and
then allow harsh words from another human or

snarled traffic or a spilled cup of coffee to ruin our entire day.

Never permit anyone, or anything, to rain on your parade. There will always be detractors, critics, or cynics who are envious of you, your skills, your work, and your way of life. Ignore them. They are like a bell at a grade crossing, clanging loudly and vainly as the train roars by. Your hours and your days are much too precious to be disturbed by this jealous group who never see a good quality in any human and yet never fail to see a bad one. They are human owls, vigilant in darkness and blind to the light, mousing for vermin but never seeing noble game.

No one can ever distract you from being happy and doing your best . . . unless you give them permission to do so. Remember that he who can suppress a moment's anger may prevent a day of sorrow.

The little misfortunes and stinging remarks of each day, if dwelled upon and magnified, can do you great harm, but if you ignore and dismiss them from your mind, they will gradually lose all their force. Detractors are everywhere. Remember that envy, like the worm, is always attracted to the fairest apple. Franklin once said that those who despair to rise in distinction by their own efforts are happy if others can be depressed to a level with themselves.

You cannot make progress in your life as a hermit, and so you must make contact with the world and its parade of misfortunes and critics, yet you need never allow either to rain on your parade. Turn away from the envious.

Never return their envy and venom with your own heat. Remember that kindling a fire for your enemy is like burning down your own home to get rid of a rat. Never stoop to his level. Booker T. Washington, who rose from degradation and hopelessness as a slave, gave all of us a special lesson on living a better life when he wrote, "I shall allow no man to belittle my soul by making me hate him." Think of those words the next time someone tries to drag you down to his level.

Nothing external can have any power over me. Let that be your motto, as it was Walt Whitman's, and it will see you peacefully through any day.

Many years ago, early one Sunday morning, I was sitting in a Texas diner just outside El Paso, enjoying my breakfast and also being entertained by a vivacious and perky blond waitress who was smiling and joking with all of us as she rushed from table to table with her orders. Here was someone who was obviously enjoying her job and her life, and her attitude was contagious. All of us that morning felt a little better because of her.

While I was sipping my second cup of coffee, thinking of the long drive ahead, an elderly man with a bulging briefcase slumped on the next stool, took a hurried look at the menu, and waved at our little waitress. She bounced toward him, flashed her best Texas smile, and said, "It's a great day, isn't it!"

The old gent's mouth curled, and he snarled, "What's so great about it?"

The pretty blonde's smile never wavered. "Well, sir, you just try missing a few, and you'll find out!"

You control your life. If anyone rains on your parade and ruins your day, it is only because you allowed it. Never again, right?

RULE FIFTEEN
. . . for a Better Way to Live

Never allow anyone to rain on your parade and thus cast a pall of gloom and defeat on the entire day. Remember that no talent, no self-denial, no brains, no character, are required to set up in the fault-finding business. Nothing external can have any power over you unless you permit it. Your time is too precious to be sacrificed in wasted days combating the menial forces of hate, jealousy, and envy. Guard your fragile life carefully. Only God can shape a flower, but any foolish child can pull it to pieces.

XVI

RULE SIXTEEN
. . . for a Better Way to Live

Search for the seed of good in every adversity. Master that principle and you will own a precious shield that will guard you well through all the darkest valleys you must traverse. Stars may be seen from the bottom of a deep well, when they cannot be discerned from the mountaintop. So will you learn things in adversity that you would never have discovered without trouble. There is always a seed of good. Find it and prosper.

It was perhaps a year after I had been promoted to the presidency of W. Clement Stone's *Success Unlimited* magazine, and with the help of Paul Harvey's commercials, on national radio, our circulation was soaring to unexplored heights on the sales chart in my office. And then I made a terrible error in judgment, an error that was certain not only to slow our progress but cost our company a fortune.

As soon as I realized what I had done, I phoned W. Clement Stone and asked for a meeting, where

I carefully spelled out, with no punches pulled, how I had managed to foul things up. Mr. Stone listened carefully to my words, interrupting only a few times to clarify certain facts, and when I finished, I just sat there, feeling I had let him down, and waited for the ax to fall. My publishing career, I was certain, was over.

Mr. Stone continued to study the ceiling, drawing on his long Havana cigar many times, before he finally turned toward me, smiling, and said, "That's terrific, Og!"

Terrific? Had the man lost his mind? I had just cost him a small fortune while jeopardizing his beloved magazine, and he was telling me it was terrific! I said nothing, probably because I was in partial shock. Then Mr. Stone leaned forward, touched my arm, and said softly, "That really is terrific, Og. Let me explain why."

The great man then proceeded to teach me a rule to live by that has been invaluable to me over the past quarter-century. Carefully, he explained that although he realized that what had happened to the magazine was a terrible adversity, he was certain that if we looked long and hard at our problem, we would find a seed of good in all that trouble, a seed that we could turn to our advantage. He reminded me that whenever God shut one door, another was always opened, and for the next several hours we discussed our problem, from every possible aspect. Finally, as I took pages of notes, we worked out a plan that not only eventually recovered our heavy loss but added greatly to our advertising revenue for many years. Those special hours were the greatest learning experience of my life.

Always search for the seed of good in every

adversity. There is no tougher rule to live by, and yet, after you have trained yourself to react to any problem with the words "That's terrific!" and then take the time to discover what could possibly be beneficial about your serious problem, you will be amazed at how often you will turn certain defeat into victory.

Samuel Smiles, who wrote the first success book, entitled *Self-Help,* in the late nineteenth century, said that we always learn more from our failures than from our successes. We often discover what will do by finding out what will not do, and he who never made a mistake has never known the thrill of turning apparent loss into a gain.

The principle of making assets out of liabilities is as old as man. Consider Santa's friends, the Eskimos, who have managed to survive for millennia by extracting the seed of good from their greatest adversity. They convert the only raw materials available to them, ice and snow, into igloos to keep them warm. An old golfing friend of mine says that the real test in life, as in golf, is not in keeping out of the rough but in getting out after we've hit one in the tall grass. Championships, in games and in life, are won by those who have learned to cope with adversity.

RULE SIXTEEN
. . . for a Better Way to Live

Search for the seed of good in every adversity. Master that principle and you will own a precious shield that will guard you well through all the darkest valleys you must traverse. Stars may be seen from the bottom of a deep well, when they cannot be discerned from the mountaintop. So will you learn things in adversity that you would never have discovered without trouble. There is always a seed of good. Find it and prosper.

XVII

RULE SEVENTEEN
. . . for a Better Way to Live

Realize that true happiness lies within you. Waste no time and effort searching for peace and contentment and joy in the world outside. Remember that there is no happiness in having or in getting, but only in giving. Reach out. Share. Smile. Hug. Happiness is a perfume you cannot pour on others without getting a few drops on yourself.

Nathaniel Hawthorne warned us, long ago, that it was much easier to capture a butterfly than that elusive feeling called happiness. Happiness, he wrote, when it comes in this world, comes incidentally. Make it the object of pursuit and it will lead you on a wild-goose chase and never be attained. And yet, as Aristotle declared to the world, "Happiness is the meaning and purpose of life, the whole aim and end of human existence."

Consider the hordes gathering in the cities each evening, searching for a few hours of happiness. How many millions of dollars do we spend, each year, purchasing pleasure of all sorts? Does it work? Are we happy? Recently, I conducted a small experiment that I had been talking about doing for years. One sunny afternoon I took up a position on the corner of Fifth Avenue and Fifty-fourth Street in New York City and checked the next two hundred people who passed me, heading south. As I expected, less than ten were smiling, or even looking happy. Why? If happiness is a normal state, like good health, why aren't more of us enjoying it?

We're probably not enjoying it because we're not even certain what it is. Most of us assume that if we had great wealth or power, we would certainly be happy, and yet I know several very tormented and lonely millionaires. Recently, on a fascinating cruise through the Panama Canal on the *Royal Princess*, I was amazed at how few happy faces were on board this elegant luxury liner. Being pampered, waited on, and spoiled seemed to make no difference to most of the passengers. I should not have been surprised. If the ingredients for happiness are not within a person, no material success or entertainment or platinum credit cards can make that person smile.

Thoreau, my old friend, had much to say on this subject, including, "I am convinced, from experience, that to maintain oneself on this earth is not a hardship but a pastime, if we will live simply and wisely. Most of the luxuries, and many of the so-called comforts of life, are not only dispensable, but positive hindrances to the elevation of mankind."

Remember the White Knight in Lewis Carroll's *Through the Looking Glass*? When Alice met the old boy, he was loaded down with luxuries—a beehive to capture bees that might approach him, a mousetrap to protect him from rodents, anklets around his horse's feet to guard against shark bites, and even a dish in anticipation of the plum pudding that some kind soul might offer him. Laden down with gadgets, the knight is a perfect symbol of those who seek happiness by collecting money and objects and real estate.

Happiness . . . a butterfly? Maybe not. "Very little is needed to make a happy life," wrote Marcus Aurelius, "it is all within yourself, in your way of thinking." You will search for happiness forever, and fail, unless you look for it within yourself, within your own heart and soul, and then share what you possess with no thought of any reward. Listen to George Eliot. "It is only a poor sort of happiness that could ever come by caring very much about our own narrow pleasures. We can only have the highest happiness such as goes along with true greatness by having wide thoughts and much feeling for the rest of the world as well as ourselves. This special sort of happiness often brings so much pain with it that we can only tell it from pain by its being what we would choose above everything else, because our souls see that it is good."

It's good to have money and the things that money can buy, but it's good, too, to check up once in a while and make sure you haven't lost the things that money can't buy.

Reach out to others. Happiness is only a by-product of how you treat your fellow man. The time to be happy is now. The place to be happy is here. Learn and begin living the rules that have been delivered to you, rules presented to you with much love, and share their message with others pleading for your support. Only then will the butterfly come and light on your shoulder while the music box plays. There never was, nor will there ever be, a better way to live.

RULE SEVENTEEN
. . . for a Better Way to Live

Realize that true happiness lies within you. Waste no time and effort searching for peace and contentment and joy in the world outside. Remember that there is no happiness in having or in getting, but only in giving. Reach out. Share. Smile. Hug. Happiness is a perfume you cannot pour on others without getting a few drops on yourself.

EPILOGUE

Farewell. I shall miss you, but our special friendship need never end. If you wish, you can keep me close by *as long as you live,* providing you learn and then put into practice the Rules for a Better Way to Live. I'd like that very much.

I hope that you have enjoyed your visits with me as much as I've enjoyed having you here, in my studio. Byron wrote that all farewells should be sudden, and maybe he was correct, but the truth of the matter is that I really don't want to see you walk out of this room for the last time. We have accomplished so much together . . . and of course there's more to be done.

I've always had a terrible time, through the

years, leaving precious friends behind or having them move away. It took many months for the pain to subside when my sons, first Dana and later Matt, finally flew away from the nest.

I'm afraid I anguish almost as much about parting with inanimate objects to which I have become attached. I still have an old Stereo-Realist camera that takes three-dimensional slides no photography studio will any longer process, golf clubs with wooden shafts, some very wide neckties, and an old 1974 white Cadillac Eldorado convertible that has been my primary set of "wheels" for the past fifteen years.

And so, like a scene from an old black-and-white movie, here I am standing in the station, still waving at your vanishing train and thinking of so much more that I could have said to you. Yet I know so well from experience that in the final showdown your future is strictly up to you. No book, no lecture, no seminar, no teacher, coach, priest, minister, or rabbi, and no motivational tape, can do anything toward altering the way you live unless *you* are determined to pay the price in time and effort and sacrifice and pain. The choice is yours . . . and yours alone.

What is past is past. You can do nothing about yesterday and last month and the failures of last year, but you can do everything toward making tomorrow and the rest of your life what you have always dreamed it could be. For you, the best is ahead, providing you follow the Rules, and now that you know about my past, I'll wager you will agree that if Og Mandino can make it, anybody can make it . . . certainly *you*! No more excuses and alibis, okay?

There is indeed a better way to live . . . and

now you have the keys. Use them. Don't let me down. More important, don't let yourself down!

Good-bye, my special friend. May the Lord watch between me and thee, when we are absent, one from another.

Mizpah!

Og Mandino

ABOUT THE AUTHOR

OG MANDINO is the most widely read inspirational and self-help author in the world today. His fourteen books have sold more than twenty-five million copies in eighteen languages. Thousands of people from all walks of life have openly credited Og Mandino with turning their lives around and for the miracle they have found in his words. His books of wisdom, inspiration, and love include *A Better Way to Live; The Choice; The Christ Commission; The Gift of Acabar; The Greatest Miracle in the World; The Greatest Salesman in the World; The Greatest Salesman in the World, Part II: The End of the Story; The Greatest Secret in the World; The Greatest Success in the World; Mission: Success!; Og Mandino's University of Success; and The Return of the Ragpicker.*